977.503　　　　　　　　　　152510
  Smi

        Smith.
        Observations on the Wisconsin
          Territory.

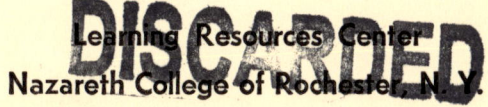

Learning Resources Center
Nazareth College of Rochester, N.Y.

MID-AMERICAN
★ FRONTIER ★

This is a volume in the Arno Press collection

MID-AMERICAN ★ FRONTIER ★

Advisory Editor
Jerome O. Steffen

Editorial Board
Richard S. Brownlee
William W. Savage, Jr.

*See last pages of this volume
for a complete list of titles*

OBSERVATIONS

ON THE

WISCONSIN TERRITORY

[William Rudolph Smith]

LEARNING RESOURCES CENTER
NAZARETH COLLEGE

ARNO PRESS
A New York Times Company
New York – 1975

Editorial Supervision: ANDREA HICKS

Reprint Edition 1975 by Arno Press Inc.

Reprinted from a copy in The State
  Historical Society of Wisconsin Library

THE MID-AMERICAN FRONTIER
ISBN for complete set: 0-405-06845-X
See last pages of this volume for titles.

Manufactured in the United States of America

<u>Publisher's Note</u>: The map facing title page
has been reproduced in black and white in
this edition.

Library of Congress Cataloging in Publication Data

Smith, William Rudolph, 1787-1868.
    Observations on the Wisconsin Territory.

    (The Mid-American frontier)
    Reprint of the 1838 ed. published by E. L. Carey and
A. Hart, Philadelphia.
    1. Wisconsin--Description and travel. 2. Frontier
and pioneer life--Wisconsin. I. Title. II. Series.
F585.S66 1975   977.5'03   75-122
ISBN 0-405-06887-5

OBSERVATIONS

ON THE

WISCONSIN TERRITORY;

CHIEFLY ON THAT PART CALLED

THE

"WISCONSIN LAND DISTRICT."

WITH

A MAP,

EXHIBITING THE SETTLED PARTS

OF THE

TERRITORY,

As laid off in Counties by Act of the Legislature in 1837.

PHILADELPHIA:
E. L. CAREY & A. HART.
1838.

Entered according to the Act of Congress, A. D. 1838, in the Clerk's Office of the District Court for the Eastern District of Pennsylvania.

E. G. DORSEY, PRINTER,
LIBRARY STREET

PRELIMINARY.

The following observations are merely a compilation of the contents of a series of letters, divested of epistolary form, addressed to Richard Penn Smith, Esq., of Philadelphia, giving the impressions of the writer, as received during a short residence in, and occasional rambles through, that part of Wisconsin Territory known as the "Wisconsin Land District," in the summer of 1837.

By the desire of a few friends, who have considered the remarks worthy of being made public, the writer has consented to have them thus sent forth in a form that claims no other merit than that of being the result of personal views, and of those feelings in regard to a country so little known as Wisconsin, which so beautiful and interesting a region would naturally suggest on a first visit.

If his fellow citizens in the east may in

any measure be gratified in perusing these observations, or should they eventually be conducive to the settlement and interests of the "lovely land of Wisconsin," the writer will be amply rewarded. The indulgence of the public must be accorded to brief accounts and hasty details, embodied in private letters written to a brother. The notes have been added lately, to explain or corroborate the views of the writer.

WM. R. SMITH.

CONTENTS.

WISCONSIN, - - - - - - - PAGE 1
Boundaries of the Wisconsin Land District—Limits of Excursions—First Impressions—Rich Country—Disadvantages—Timber, scarcity for building purposes, how to be remedied—Price of Lumber—Pine of the Mississippi—Climate—Corn Crops—Dry Winters—Wheat, Spring and Fall Sowing—Cold Winds—Planting Trees, advantages to the Farmer—Price of Land—Rich Soil—Produce of Crops—Various Productions—The Wisconsin Potato—Sugar Beet—Mining and Agricultural Interests—High Prices—Necessaries of Life—Reflections—General Description—Prairies—Groves—Fruits—Nuts—Beauty of the Country—Flowers—Mineral Plant, its Qualities—Rosin Weed or Prairie Sun-flower, its Peculiarities—Wild Indigo—Summer and Autumn Flowers—Hills—Sinsinawa Mounds—Platte Mounds—Blue Mounds—Limestone—Numerous Springs—Natural Meadows—Streams—Fish, varieties—Game, Deer, Elk, Prairie Hens, Pheasants, Partridges, Turkeys—Wolves, Prairie Wolf—Rabbits—Rattlesnakes, Prairie Rattlesnake—Interesting Query—Ancient Cultivation—Old Corn Fields—Denuded State of the Prairies, Inquiry into its cause—Character of the Prairies—No Swamp—Healthy Region, Causes—Emigration—Black Hawk War—Miners of Wisconsin—Col. Dodge—Rapid Progress of the Country—Travelling Menagerie—Western side of the Mississippi—New Territory.

vi   CONTENTS.

PRAIRIE DU CHIEN, - - - - - - 35

Pike's-hill—Mouth of Wisconsin—Prairie—Cordon on the Bluffs—Height of the River—Pére Hennepin's Travels—Fort Crevecœur—Checagou—Query—Fort Crawford—New Town—Court-house—Rev. D. Lowry—Congregation—Early Settlers—Half Breeds—Old Town—Old Fort of Prairie du Chien—American Fur Company's Warehouse—Farms of the Old Settlers—Soil and Productions—New City—Importance—Bluffs—Limit of Territory—Hospitality.

THE MILITARY ROAD, - - - - - - 43

Brunet's Ferry—Wisconsin River—Steamboat Science—Towns on the River, Sutherland, Buchanan—Blue River—La Fayette—River Trade—Brooklyn—Natural Meadows—Beautiful Scenery—Woods—Great Prairie—Hincklin's—Rich Country—Parish's—Lead Diggings—New Furnace—Fine Farm—Wingville—Pedlar's Creek Diggings—Groceries—Diamond Grove—Terry's—Bequette's—Road to Mineral Point—Dodgeville—Governor's Residence—Great Road—Farms on the Prairie—Messersmith's—Numerous Farms—Blue Mounds—Brigham's—Splendid view—Moundville—Old Fort—Grave of Lieut. Force—Interesting Anecdote.

THE FOUR LAKES, - - - - - - 55

Numerous Mounds—Fine Prairie—Large body of Wood—River of the Four Lakes—City of Madison—The Fourth Lake—Catfish River—Beauty of the Fourth Lake—Fish—Stones—Seat of Government—Extension of the City—Various names—Rapid progress—Public Buildings—Canal—First Lake—Question as to Location of Seat of Government—Additions to Madison—Public Improvements—City of the Four Lakes—Canal to Wisconsin river—Illinois Improvements in Rock river—Great Advantages of Situation—Superb Scenery—Stage Coach—Fort Winnebago—Canal—Portage—Communication with the Atlantic—Happy tendency to Union.

CONTENTS.

THE BURIAL MOUNDS, - - - - - 69

Form, composition, examination of one; conjectures; no tradition; attempts to account therefor—Pére Lafitau's work—Feast of the Dead—Conjectures—Indian customs—Stone Mounds—Pottery.

HELENA, - - - - - - - 75

Roads—Face of the Country—Splendid Amphitheatre of Meadow—Hay-makers—Feelings of a Traveller—Wisconsin River—United States Store House—Town of Helena—Shot Tower Establishment—New Store House—Description of the Shot Tower—Extensive View—Indian Country.

MINERAL POINT, - - - - - - - 81

Description—Population—Distances—Executive and County Offices—Stores and Taverns—Buildings—Miners' Dwellings—Fine Spring—Additions to the Town—Mechanics—Miners—High Wages—Town Surveyed—Settlers' Claims—Country around—Mine Holes—Mineral Lands—Galena—Course of the Lead Trade—Miner and Smelter—Profit—Copper Mines—Great Product of the Diggings—Richness of the Ore—Value of the Mines.

BELMONT, - - - - - - - 90

Road from Mineral Point—Peketonica—Great Prairie—Fine farms—Platte Mounds—Belmont—Town and Country—Description of the Mounds—Race Course—Beautiful and extensive view—Interesting picture—Platte Village and Mills.

THE PEKETONICA OR PEE-KE-TOL-I-KA, - - - 96

New Baltimore—M'Kim's Furnace and establishment—Extent of the river—Wiota—Rich Meadows—Cedar Bluffs—Willow Springs—Public Roads—Farms—Bracken's—Sheldon's—Hospitalities—Intelligence of the Settlers—Books and Newspapers—Lead diggings—The Indian Reservations—

CONTENTS.

Claims by Improvement—Otterbourne—Gratiot—The Peketonica Country—Hamilton—Indian Town—Rock River Improvements.

ELK GROVE, - - - - - - - 104
Highly cultivated Farms—Clinton—Advantages of Elk Grove—Prairies.

GALENA, - - - - - - - - 106
Fevre River—Importance of Galena—Great trade—Ferry—Description of the Town—Steamboats—Newspapers of Wisconsin Territory.

STATISTICS AND OBSERVATIONS, - - - - 110
Population of the Territory—Western Wisconsin—Spirit of Speculation—Counties in the Territory—Wisconsin Land District—Legislature—Executive—Secretary—Judiciary—Appointments of Officers of Government, Salaries—Delegate to Congress—Appropriation for Public Buildings—Education Funds—Towns on the right bank of the Mississippi—Distance from St. Louis, and Population—Distance from Pittsburg to the Falls of St. Anthony—Towns on the left bank of the Mississippi—Distance from St. Louis and Population—Post Offices in the Territory.

CASSVILLE, - - - - - - - 123

IOWA TERRITORY, - - - - - - 125

WISCONSIN.

Boundaries of the Wisconsin Land District—Limits of Excursions—First Impressions—Rich Country—Disadvantages—Timber, scarcity for building purposes, how to be remedied—Price of Lumber—Pine of the Mississippi—Climate—Corn Crops—Dry Winters—Wheat, Spring and Fall Sowing—Cold Winds—Planting Trees, advantages to the Farmer—Price of Land—Rich Soil—Produce of Crops—Various Productions—The Wisconsin Potato—Sugar Beet—Mining and Agricultural Interests—High Prices—Necessaries of Life—Reflections—General Description—Prairies—Groves—Fruits—Nuts—Beauty of the Country—Flowers—Mineral Plant, its Qualities—Rosin Weed or Prairie Sun-flower, its Peculiarities—Wild Indigo—Summer and Autumn Flowers—Hills—Sinsinawa Mounds—Platte Mounds—Blue Mounds—Limestone—Numerous Springs—Natural Meadows—Streams—Fish, varieties—Game, Deer, Elk, Prairie Hens, Pheasants, Partridges, Turkeys—Wolves, Prairie Wolf—Rabbits—Rattlesnakes, Prairie Rattlesnake—Interesting Query—Ancient Cultivation—Old Corn Fields—Denuded State of the Prairies, Inquiry into its cause—Character of the Prairies—No Swamp—Healthy Region, Causes—Emigration—Black Hawk War—Miners of Wisconsin—Col. Dodge—Rapid progress of the Country—Travelling Menagerie—Western side of the Mississippi—New Territory.

A RESIDENCE of two months in Wisconsin Territory, and almost daily excursions in various parts of what is properly called the Wisconsin Land District, have in some measure enabled me to comply with the request, of giving you an outline of the country, its productions, and its agricultural advantages.

This Land District is bounded westward by the Mississippi, east by the Four Lakes and Sugar river, north by the Wisconsin river, and south by the Illinois state line, comprising an extent of country about ninety miles from east to west, and about fifty miles from north to south, generally covered by the counties of Iowa, Grant, Dane and Green. The country lying east of this section, is called the Milwaukie Land District, and embraces all the remaining counties of the Territory except those on the western side of the Mississippi river.

In order that you may the better understand the localities of my journeyings and observations, cast your eyes on Mitchell's or Tanner's latest maps of the United States, or if you can procure Judson's or Hathaway's map of Wisconsin, they are the best, being accurately copied from the plats in the land office,* and trace a line from Prairie du Chien eastward and south of the Wisconsin river, until you reach the head of the Fourth lake, a distance of about ninety miles, and this is the extent of my travel from west to east; then trace a line from Helena on

* Messrs. Hinman & Dutton, of Philadelphia, have lately published an accurate map of Wisconsin, with the new counties laid off; this map is attached to the work, although the text has not been altered.

the Wisconsin river south to the Illinois State line, and give an allowance for various excursions into the country, on both sides of these two principal lines, particularly in and about the mineral region, and the head waters of the Peketonica, or Pee-kee-tol-i-ka, and you have my daily whereabout during my stay in the Territory; consequently you will apply my remarks on soil and productions principally to these sections of the country.

First impressions with regard to a new country, where every thing appears different from what one has been accustomed to see, are always apt to please, whether the country be wild, rugged, rocky and mountainous, or composed of level plains, denuded sand hills, and wide expanses of inland waters: such is the character of many parts of the great West, and even here, the first view pleases, not only from its novelty of scenery, but, abstracted from the idea of its utility to the various wants and occupations of man, no country in a state of nature can be unpleasing to the reflecting mind; no object on which the eye may not for a moment dwell satisfied, not even the coral rock in the midst of the ocean. If such scenes may please, what then may you conceive first impressions to be with regard to Wisconsin, when I tell you that fancy must fail in imagining a more lovely country: the agriculturist in vain might seek for a richer or more productive soil; the mineralogist fruitlessly explore the bowels of the earth to discover veins of lead, copper, (and from many specimens, I believe also of iron,) richer than in Wisconsin!*

* The following note is an extract from Schoolcraft's remarks on the lead mine country on the upper Mississippi, addressed to the Editors of the New York Mirror.

"The angle formed by the junction of the Wisconsin with the Mississippi, is a sombre line of weather-beaten rocks. Gliding along the current at the base of these rocks, the idea of a "hill country" of no very productive character, is naturally impressed upon the observer, and this impression came down probably from the days of Marquette, who was the first European that we read of who descended the Wisconsin, and became the true discoverer of the Mississippi. The fact that it yielded lead ore, bits of which were occasionally brought in by the natives, was in accordance with this opinion; and aided it may be supposed in keeping out of view the real character of the country. I know not how else to account for the light which has suddenly burst upon us from this bank of the Mississippi, and which has at once proved it to be as valuable for the purpose of agriculture as for those of mining, and as sylvan in its appearance as if it were not fringed, as it were, with rocks, and lying at a great elevation above the water. This elevation is so considerable as to permit a lively descent in the streams, forming numerous mill seats. The surface of the country is not, however, broken, but may be compared to the *heavy and lazy rolling waves of the sea after a tempest*. These wave-like plains are often destitute of trees, except a few scattering ones, but present to the eye an almost boundless field of native herbage. Groves of oak sometimes diversify these native meadows, or cover the ridges which bound them. Very rarely does any rock appear above the surface. The highest elevations, the Platte Mounds and the Blue Mounds are covered with soil and with trees. Numerous brooks of limpid water traverse the plains, and find their way into either the Wisconsin, Rock river, or the Mississippi. The common deer is still in possession of its favourite haunts; and the traveller is very

This unqualified picture of wealth in the new country, you may think is too strongly drawn; I cannot help it—such were my first impressions of the Territory; they have been the more realized, the more I have travelled in it, and the more information I have obtained. I appeal fearlessly to every person who has been three days in any quarter of the Wisconsin Land District for the truth of my assertions; I believe from all that I have seen, that there is not to be found ten acres in any one hundred that is not fit for cultivation or for the farmer's use. No one can say where mineral is *not to be found;* wherever it has been properly sought for, it has been obtained; and even around Mineral Point, where are the richest lead diggings, and as poor a soil as any that I have seen in the Territory, the land will produce equal to any land in Pennsylvania with proper and equal cultivation. Mineral is also found in the *richest* agricultural districts, and under the finest

often startled by flocks of the prairie hen, rising up in his path. The surface soil is a rich, black alluvion; it yields abundant crops of corn, and so far as they have been tried, all the cereal gramina. I have never, either in the west or out of the west, seen a richer soil, or more stately fields of corn and oats, than upon one of the plateaux of the Blue Mound.

Such is the country which appears to be richer in ores of lead than any other mineral district in the world—which yielded forty millions of pounds in seven years—produced a single lump of ore of two thousand cubic feet—and appears adequate to supply almost any amount of this article that the demands of commerce require.

1*

soil in the Territory. The disadvantages attending the farmer in such a rich agricultural country must of course be very few, and I shall point them out, I trust with candour.

In the first place there is a want of timber; in many sections of this country there is abundance of timber for building, fencing, firewood, coaling, and all other purposes; yet generally speaking, in the rich prairies, the groves of timber are small and scattered, not affording sufficient wood for more than one or two large farms, for many miles in extent. Yet this want of timber can be easily remedied by planting the yellow, the white or the black locust, and the chestnut; these trees are not indigenous; the general forest trees are white oak, burr oak, hickory, black and white walnut, sugar maple, cherry and ash. I am told that locust and chestnut flourish well by planting the seed; and if the farmer on the prairies will turn his attention to throwing up of embankments, and thereon planting thorn hedges, which in many places I have seen commenced, the want of fencing timber can scarcely be felt: as for fire wood, a sufficiency may always be readily obtained within a short distance of any farm; and if the annual fires on the prairies are prevented or subdued by the care and exertions of the settlers, the timber of the country is of the most rapid growth. Thus, the objection of the scarcity of timber has more force in name than in reality, when the rapid growth of plantations, the easy cultivation of hedges, and the spontaneous production of indigenous forest trees, where fire is excluded in the prairies, are properly reflected upon.

But the objection presents itself with more force in regard to lumber for building purposes. As for oak, walnut, cherry and ash, and on the river, the cottonwood, and in some parts the sugar-maple, there is abundance for the heavy parts of buildings; but pine lumber is scarce, and of course dear; even the ordinary lumber of the country commands now two dollars per hundred feet at the saw-mills; this is owing to the scarcity of saw-mills, and the consequent increased demand for the article. There is no pine timber in the country, except very high up the Wisconsin river, above Fort Winnebago, and up the St. Croix river, and the other tributaries of the upper Mississippi. Pine lumber is worth six dollars per hundred at Prairie du Chien, Cassville, and Galena, in Illinois; these towns may be called the chief shipping ports of this part of Wisconsin territory. Pine lumber is brought down the Ohio river from the tributaries of the Allegheny above Pittsburg, as far up as the New York state line, and taken up the Mississippi by way of St. Louis; and instances have occurred of houses having been built altogether at Pittsburgh, and at Cincinnati, and shipped *in parts* around to the territory, and placed on the ground cheaper than they could have been built by procuring the lumber from the Wisconsin river or the upper Mississippi. The late treaty made with the Chippewas, by which the pine region has been purchased by the United States, will hereafter ensure a constant supply of building material, and greatly reduce its price in Wisconsin, and along the Mississippi to St. Louis, and even as far as New Orleans. Saw-mills are already being established within the purchase.

Another objection, and the main one to be considered, is the climate: as I have not passed a spring or winter month here, I give such information as I have obtained. The winter is long and severe, and yet the general temperature of the atmosphere is not colder than it is amongst the mountains in Western Pennsylvania. The utmost duration of winter may be considered as of five months; this will include two months of wet and cold season in the spring and fall not properly called winter. From the beginning of May, until the end of October, the climate of this region to a Pennsylvanian is delightful. I can say for myself, that I never experienced *hotter* weather than in some days in August, in Wisconsin; this is generally the case in high northern latitudes. During the greater portion of the summer months, however warm may be some days, yet the general character is that of a temperature of 75° to 80° Fahrenheit. Frost commences in the middle of September generally; vicissitudes of climate which bring frosts destructive to grain early in September, are not uncommon in Pennsylvania in the same month; nay, as early as the 25th of August, in the northwestern part of that state, I have seen whole crops of corn and buckwheat destroyed. But the frosts of September seldom injure the corn crops in Wisconsin. Corn is undoubtedly considered as more uncertain than any other crop here, and yet if attention were paid to the quality of the *seed corn* as regards *nativity* and *first ripening*, I have no doubt that this highly favoured country may in time be as fine a corn growing region as any in our land. Understand me; as to *nativity*, I mean that the seed corn should be brought from our middle and northern states, and not from Kentucky, Missouri, and the south part of Illinois and Indiana; and as to *first ripening*, the farmer's chief care should be to select the *earliest* ears for seed. By this mode of planting and selecting, and in its continuance, I make no question that corn may be acclimated, improved, and rendered a *certain* crop. In some parts of the eastern district of Wisconsin, I have been informed that the corn crop has been matured in ten weeks from its being planted.

Continuing my remarks on the winters, I understand, that when the cold weather has fairly set in, the snows fall, although by no means deep; snows continue to fall at intervals, until the winter is about to break up: there is no rain of any amount known to fall from October, until March or April. The cold is severe and the weather dry: no melting of the snow, no rains injurious to cattle, no wet, *sloppy* time occurs in the winter, to occasion wet feet and drenched clothes, to the farmer and traveller, with all the host of colds, coughs, rheumatism, and consequent ills that attend on a variable winter. Winter is here, to be sure in *earnest*, and yet not colder than in the same latitudes eastward; and when his icy hand is lifted from the locked up land, you leap as with a bound at once into delightful summer.*

---

* Since the above remarks were written, I find the following paragraph in one of the newspapers of the territory.

Du Buque, W. T., Dec. 25, 1837.

To the Editors of the Iowa News.

Gentlemen:—For the information of some of your eastern readers, many of whom entertain the most erroneous ideas in regard to the climate of Wisconsin, please to do me the favour to publish the following facts, affording an opportunity of forming a comparison between their winters and ours. Snow fell to the depth of a few inches at Franklin, Venango county, Pa. on the 17th of October last. It snowed in Philadelphia during the whole of the 14th of November last.

The Blairsville (Pa.) Record of the 15th of November ult. says, "The mountain ridges in sight of this town, are now, the second time this fall, whitened with snow.

There was not a particle of snow seen this season at Du Buque until November the 22nd, when we had a fall of about one and a half inches, which, however, immediately disappeared.

Steamboats continued to arrive here until the 8th of this month, (Dec.) and might have done so considerably longer, as the Mississippi did not freeze over until the 21st inst.

On the night of the 14th December, our first *permanent* snow

Spring wheat is here generally raised, and the reason given why the fall sowing does not equally prosper with the spring sowing, is the length and severity of the winter, and the want of protection for the grain on the prairies, over which the winds have almost unbounded sweep, and consequently drive the snow from its genial covering on the tender plant. Now, although this may be all true, yet remedies are to be found. Let us say to the farmer, sow your wheat early in September, and the plant will have gained sufficient strength to resist the evils complained of: the custom of October sowing, as prevailing in Pennsylvania, will not do in Wisconsin. If it were necessary to produce facts to prove a self-evident theory, I have been informed of two or three similar instances which substantiate it. Winter wheat was *stubbled* in, after a corn crop had been taken off; the stalks of corn, some standing and

commenced falling, and continued until it reached a depth of six or eight inches, affording us delightful sleighing. I have never known the snow to exceed eight inches since I have been in Wisconsin, and am assured on good authority, that it has rarely, if ever, been seen here any deeper.

The winters here are remarkably pleasant, being peculiarly dry, clear, and uniform in temperature. At the beginning of this month, our farmers were busily engaged in *ploughing* around Du Buque. Will some of your brother editors at the east have the goodness to inform us whether any of their neighbours were similarly occupied in *December*.

I am, very respectfully, your ob't serv't,

JOHN PLUMBE, Jr.

some fallen, afforded such a protection as to retain the snow on the wheat during the winter; a fine crop was the result. But this may be called slovenly farming; early sowing is the remedy, or rather preventive, of the effect of severe winters.

These appear to me as the prominent objections to the agricultural interests in Wisconsin; want of timber, coldness of climate, and length of winter. I have merely suggested some hints of the manner in which these objections may be obviated. Personal feeling, in the coldness of the country, is scarcely worthy of consideration; a family can be as easily kept most comfortably warm in winter, in Wisconsin, as in New York or Pennsylvania, and the absence of winter coughs, and colds destructive to the human system will amply compensate for a thousand *icy* inconveniences.

One further remark on the winter climate. The situation of this territory being west of the great lakes of the north west, the freezing and biting winds, which prevail in parts of New York and Pennsylvania during the winter, deriving their character chiefly in passing over the immense waste of frozen lakes, have no effect in Wisconsin; and when the prairies become settled by farmers who will turn their attention to the planting and preserving of fruit and forest trees, I have no doubt that the climate will still more be meliorated, in every succeeding year, with the settlement of the country.

The advantages of the agriculturist, now, at least, greatly overbalance all his inconveniences. His land is purchased at the government price of one dollar and twenty-five cents per acre: land of the richest soil in the world. His prairie ground awaits immediate cultivation. His crops will yield him from thirty-five to fifty bushels of fall wheat per acre, and from twenty to thirty bushels of spring wheat is calculated on as a sure crop; barley will yield from forty to sixty bushels, and oats from fifty to seventy-five bushels to the acre, corn will produce from forty to sixty bushels, and potatoes, turnips, rutabaga and all garden vegetables yield most abundantly. Potatoes of a quality and size superior to any I have ever tasted, yield from three hundred to five hundred bushels to the acre; and with regard to this vegetable, I venture to predict, that the time will arrive when the Wisconsin potato, *par excellence,* will become an article of trade in the best demand in the southern markets. I am satisfied that this country is *peculiarly* adapted to the cultivation of the sugar beet; and add to all these advantages the certainty of a ready, and high priced market, and there is every inducement for agricultural pursuits. The only *evil* to be feared is that the farmer may strike his plough into a lead vein, and then *adieu* to the plough and the harrow, and *welcome* the pick-axe, and the crow-bar, the windlass, and the new smelting furnace; the prospect of a *mineral* fortune is opened to the farmer at once, and he cannot resist the temptation of improving it.

The mining and agricultural interests of this country, must always depend greatly on each other; they must flourish together, their mutual interests require their mutual protection. The mining interest always finds the farmer a ready market. The miner attends to his own business exclusively; he does not meddle with the soil except to see what lies beneath it; he very seldom even cultivates a garden; this fact, and the constant tide of emigration creating a demand far exceeding the supply every year, causes the price of produce to be astonishingly high, one dollar per bushel for oats, and the same for potatoes, corn, onions, turnips and beets was paid when I was at Mineral Point; I am informed that the prices are seldom twenty-five per cent below this average. The high price of wheat all over the Union for a year past is no general criterion, and yet flour is always high here, which is partly owing to the present scarcity of grist mills.

The necessaries and the luxuries of life, the various articles of household furniture, and every description of farming implements can be readily procured in the Territory, as the steamboats are daily arriving and departing, at the several points of shipment on the Mississippi, and the price of carriage is regulated according to the stage of the water and the number of boats plying on the river.

Enough, I hear you say, of this talk, desultory and conjectural concerning the farming of Wisconsin; let us hear more of the country; its general appearance, its waters, its hills, its woods, and its vallies; its aboriginal remains, its towns, and their population; its lead and its copper; and write to me like a traveller who journies, and wishes to impart what he has seen, in a country so recently rescued by the enterprise and valor of our hardy pioneers, from the wandering Indian, whose only occupation was to hunt deer and spear fish, although dwelling in a Western Eden.

Be it so: I will endeavour to comply with all you ask, but before I commence, an observation rises in my mind, to which I feel that I must give utterance. It is not inconsistent with the wise and bountiful orders and dispensations of our Creator, to believe whilst viewing this beautiful country, that its fertility of soil, and its facility of being cultivated, may have been adapted to the capabilities of its primitive inhabitants. Such a soil as we here find would yield abundance to a people, who might be ignorant of the mechanical arts, and although I have no morbid sensibility on the subject of taking possession of a land which was worthless in the hands, and under the dominion of roving savages; and as I am of opinion that the earth was given to man for his inheritance, and consequently that the general good will justify the means by which that inheritance is claimed, yet

I cannot help seeing that if there is any country on the face of the globe where a nation might merely *exist* without the knowledge of the arts of civilized life, a country capable of affording the greatest sustenance with the least labour, such a country is to be found in the valley of the Mississippi, and such a country is now before me in Wisconsin!

There is neither mountain nor forest, (properly so called,) in Western Wisconsin, that is in the section which I have limited in my outset in these remarks. The prairies may be passed over in any direction in a wheel carriage with ease and safety; the groves surrounding, and interlacing, and sprinkling, and dotting the vast ocean of open field, can be threaded as easily with a carriage, as if you were driving through a plantation of fruit or forest trees, set or growing irregularly. The undergrowth is generally of small bushes readily passed over; the black currant, the furred and the smooth gooseberry, the red and the white raspberry, the blackberry, the cranberry of the vine, and of the bush; the haw, the wild plum, and the crabapple; all these indigenous fruits are found throughout the territory; the strawberry literally covers the prairies and the groves; and touching the size of this delicious fruit, I send you a paragraph from a Mineral Point newspaper; the fruit was measured by Major John P. Sheldon, and is not by any means of uncommon size;* the

---

* *Strawberries.*—Our prairies and hazel lands have produced,

hazle with its nut-laden branches is the most common bush in the country; acorns, black and white walnuts, and hickory nuts, are as plenty as hosts of swine may for ages desire. Indeed it is not possible to find a district of country better calculated for the raising of this description of stock, than here.

If I can by any means bring your imagination to bear on the appearance of the country generally, I will endeavour to do so. Suppose for a moment that you were placed in the midst of the most fertile and best cultivated parts of Lancaster or Chester counties in Pennsylvania; that the houses were all removed; the fences and hedges all levelled with the general surface; the grain fields all set in luxuriant grass; the strips of woodland interspersed amongst the farms, remaining as they are; suppose further that the most beautiful flowers variegated in

---

this season, an unusual quantity of this delicious fruit; and in some places which were favourable to their growth, they have equalled in size, the production of the best cultivated gardens. The following is the size of five berries taken from the top of a pail full, which were gathered in a field in the vicinity of Willow Springs:

> One $2\frac{1}{2}$ inches in circumference.
> Three $2\frac{5}{8}$ inches ,,
> One 3 inches ,,

The cultivation of the strawberry should be attended to in our territory, which in soil and latitude is so favourable to its growth. It would, (in the absence of almost every kind of cultivated fruit), well reward the little labour required to produce them in the greatest abundance and perfection.

colours, and of countless descriptions, were waving their plumed heads, with every here and there the tall *compass plant* or prairie sunflower, overtopping all; suppose such a scene in an area of fifteen, twenty or thirty miles; such is Wisconsin! and such have I generally found it in various rides and rambles, and excursions on foot, on horseback, and in *New York fashionable built* carriages, through a country into which the adventurous white pioneer first made his entry nine years ago, and which has only been free from the tread of savage feet, and the depredations of the Black Hawk war, within five years!

The flowers of the prairie are various and beautiful: I am not sufficiently a florist or botanist to class them, and generally speaking, they are not known in the eastern states as field flowers. The blue, red, white, and purple chrysanthemum are very common; a yellow flower waving and drooping like an ostrich feather, is also generally found; some varieties resembling the prince's-feather, are common; delicate snow drops, and violets, diamond sparks that "love the ground" form the carpet whence springs the plumed stem of many colours, intermingled with the *masonic* or mineral plant, and the *compass* or resin plant, or prairie sunflower. The mineral plant bears a bluish-purple flower, and is remarkable for the qualities attributed to its growth by the miners. It is said to indicate the presence of *mineral.* It sometimes spreads in spots over a large surface or ground, obscuring all but the grass beneath it; here the miner will dig with almost a certainty of striking on a lead mine. Sometimes the range of the flower's growth is in a straight, a curved, or an irregular line, indicating the range of the *crevice* mineral in the strata beneath; these indications are believed in, and relied on by many of the miners. If they be true, and the plant actually points out the location of the mineral (galena), then, as I have before observed, no one can say where mineral is not to be found, for this flowering plant is the most common in the country, and yet as its growth on different parts of the prairies is so irregular in quantity and in direction, there may be something in the peculiarity of soil covering mineral, which produces the plant; it is called by the miners *masonic*, perhaps in derision, as it *discloses* the *secret* mine.

The rosin or turpentine weed, or compass plant, deserves some notice; I have called it the prairie sun-flower, from its near resemblance to the flower so called with us, except that the flowers and the seeds are much smaller; the largest one I saw was about four inches in diameter, exclusive of the surrounding yellow leaves. The stem of this plant rises to the height of five or six feet, and when broken in any part, it exudes a white resinous fluid, which, on being exposed to the atmosphere, acquires a gummy consistence of the taste and smell of resin. But the strange peculiarity of the plant is, that its leaves invariably point north and south. In the writings of Dr. Atwater who has visited some parts of this country, I remember that he has noticed this flower, remarked its peculiarities, and has given its botanical name as belonging to the Helianthus tribe; I have not the book to refer to. The leaves are very large, firm and stiff; those nearest the root are largest, some of them about eighteen inches long, and about one foot wide, palmated and deeply indented; from the root, the leaves start out from the stem, on two sides only, at irregular distances, yet generally opposite each other, and these leaves invariably have a north and south direction. It is called the compass plant, because the Indians in the absence of trees on the vast prairies, could at all times find a guide in the leaves of the prairie sun-flower; and its resinous qualities might render it a good substitute for pine knots in giving light, and thus greatly enhance its properties to the benighted traveller. Horses and other cattle eat this plant with avidity, bite at it in travelling over the prairies, and seek it out from amidst the hay in the stable. It is remarked that the wild indigo always accompanies this plant.

A remarkable and beautiful feature in the decorations of the prairies is, that the *summer* flowers, after having for a season displayed their gorgeous variety, and turned up their faces to receive the glowing beams of the sun, as soon as autumn puts on her sober brown, and the airs of heaven breathe more mildly, they droop, die, and instantly give place to a new galaxy of fine and beautiful flowers, particularly all the varieties of the chrysanthemum, and a splendid drooping *bush* of flowers that looks as if it was covered with snow flakes; the autumn flowers are more delicate and less flaring than those of summer.

I have said that there is no mountain in this district; extensive ranges of hills are found on the Wisconsin river and in the north-east parts of the Territory, but the only hills in this quarter of the country are the Sinsinewa mounds, the seat of General George Wallace Jones, delegate to Congress, (these are near the Illinois State line,) the Platte mounds and the Blue mounds. These mounds serve as land-marks to the traveller over the prairies. The Platte and the Blue mounds are about forty-five miles apart; the former comprising three, and the latter two hills. These hills, with the exception of the centre one of the Platte mounds, are from two hundred to three hundred feet high, well covered with timber and generally capable of being cultivated to the summit. They are seen from almost every part of the Wisconsin Land District, and independent of their being of so much service to the traveller, in the absence of roads and of other land marks, they are objects of great natural beauty; for although the prairies are by no means a dead level, but on the contrary are most generally rolling and undulating, and in many instances may be termed *hilly*, yet these mounds very agreeably break, and diversify the otherwise monotonous view of prairie and grove, however luxuriant it may be in soil and vegetation.

I am disposed to believe that the general base of this country is of limestone: I judge from the fact that limestone is abundant and found in all parts of the Territory where I have been. It is discovered in small bodies of flat white stone lying on the surface of prairies, and at the points of the rolling hills, where the prairie dips into, and unites with the natural meadow. Perhaps there is not to be found any region in the United States better watered than Wisconsin. The springs rise generally in the prairies, and their locality is always indicated by the growth of the dwarf willow near and around the fountain head. The water is pure, cold, and deliciously refreshing; the springs after running over the prairies and through small ravines unite in some natural meadow from a quarter of a mile to a mile or more in width, and meander through the meadow in a stream, some three or four yards broad, and two feet deep, until in the accumulation of several streams, a fine and large navigable river is formed. These natural meadows present the most superb views of any part of the country. Interspersed with small groves; irregular in their course and shape, owing to the *jutting* points or hills of the prairie dipping into the meadow; the streams flowing in various directions over and through the low ground until they combine in some broad and deep channel; the high waving grass mingled with the field and meadow flowers, all afford a picture more varied and therefore more beautiful than the high prairie grounds. It is worthy of remark that the character of the streams is different from what might be expected in the deep rich soil of the meadows. The waters generally flow, nearly full with the banks, and the firm sandy and gravelly bottom always allows a safe fording place. Fine trout, perch, bass, catfish, eels, buffalo, muskelonge and other excellent fish are found in all the waters. I have seen the buffalo, muskelonge and catfish of enormous size brought by wagon loads to Mineral Point; they had been caught in the Peketonica, and many weighed from twenty to thirty pounds and upwards. The white fish of the lake country is a delicacy which might well be desired by the *gourmands* of the east; its flavour needs no sauce, and its richness and fatness render butter or lard useless in the dressing.

Game throughout the whole country is abundant. The deer are often seen sporting over the prairies, and in the groves and oak openings; they are frequently aroused out of the high grass, and as the rifle of the hunter has not yet sufficiently alarmed them in their secret lairs, they are in a measure less wild than in parts more densely settled; I have often seen them in my rambles, quietly gazing at the traveller, until he had passed by. Elks are still found, I am informed, on the wooded shores of the Wisconsin. The prairie hen, grouse or moorfowl, is an excellent bird; they are very numerous' and are found in families or broods; they are about the size of the common barn-door fowl, and I believe are the same bird as the Long Island grouse. Their flesh is delicious, juicy and fat; they fly heavily on the prairies and alight generally at a short distance, consequently they are easily bagged by the sportsman. Pheasants also are in great numbers, but the partridge or quail is not often met with; I saw three or four near some farms, and as this bird always follows, and attends cultivation, the flocks will certainly increase with the opening of farms, and raising of grain. Wild turkeys, I am told, are also numerous in many parts of the territory; I did not see any whilst there.

Two species of wolf are found in the western part of the territory; the grey wolf, which is common in the eastern states, and the prairie wolf; the latter is neither so large, nor so ferocious as the grey wolf, but still very destructive on game and on the stock of the farmer. Yet in so open a country as this, these animals must be extirpated or driven into the distant forests as fast as the settlements increase. I met at different times in my little excursions several of these prairie wolves; they appeared more alarmed than myself, and soon scampered off. Rabbits are also very numerous: indeed the abundance of fruit and of mast in this country affords ample subsistence to all kinds of game known in the eastern states.

Two kinds of rattle-snakes are found here; the brown and yellow rattle-snake, *crotalus horridus*, is sometimes of great size. I came across one on the banks of the Peketonica lying in my path; it measured between four and five feet in length, and at least nine inches in circumference; fortunately it was dead, killed by a traveller an hour or so before I saw it; I confess to an alarm at the time, as my feet were nearly upon it before I discovered it. I saw several others in various parts of the country, but they are not more numerous here than in the western parts of Pennsylvania. It is well known that these snakes always recede from cultivation, therefore there is no more danger to be apprehended from them here than in any other new section of country. The small black rattle-snake of the prairie is also at *this time* common; these are said to be more dangerous than their larger yellow brethren, as they are not so magnanimous as to give the preparatory warning before they strike; the same remarks, as to disappearance, before the improvements of the settler, applies to the black rattle-snake.

Can the belief be sustained by argument founded on the general appearance of the country, the burial mounds, so numerous and so extensive in size, found in all parts of the territory, and the vestiges of art, rude as they are, found in them, and in many other places, that this highly favoured region was once inhabited by a powerful nation, and even partially cultivated? It is not my inclination, neither is it in my power, in the brief space of these remarks, to enter into any discussion on the subject; the question is merely made, and it is well worthy the most enlightened mind to make deep researches in respect to this interesting subject. One matter I state as worthy of observation: In a ride which I made exploring the country on one of the head waters of Sugar River, in company with my son Dr. William A. Smith, and our friend Mr. John Messersmith, we found two long parallel mounds, which measured about two hundred and fifty paces in length. Mr. Messersmith, who resides about thirty miles from the place in question, and who had often been over the ground, informed me, that at a short distance from these mounds, there was a piece of ground which had every appearance of having been once cultivated. We drove in his carriage to the place, and as we passed over the soil, through high grass, which reached above the carriage wheels, the motion of the vehicle was similar to that of passing over the ridges of a corn field, which had been for years out of cultivation, and on which sod had grown. We got out of the carriage and examined the ground;

the ridges were parallel, as if they had been ploughed, or in some manner cultivated; they were very numerous, and constituted evidently an extensive range, in length and in breadth; we rode several hundred yards over them, and the impression was irresistible, that we were driving through an abandoned cornfield; and this field, if such it was, a very large one. The land was bottom prairie, and a ledge of high land nearly encompassed it. Can these ridges have been caused by the action of water? or where will conjecture rest when such evidence of cultivation is apparent? I have related the fact, and I leave the matter for future investigation, which I hope one day shortly to make.*

That the denuded state of the country has been caused by fire, originally, and the growth of timber kept down by the annual conflagration of the prairies, may be the truth; and yet it is also true, that in no part of the country, on the prairies, as far as I can learn, has any, even the slightest, appearance of *charred wood* been found. Surely if this country had at any former period been well wooded, and the action of fire had destroyed whole forests, where at this time

* Col. George Davenport of Rock Island, informs me, that in the year 1823, some Winnebago Indians found on the Peketonica, a *cannon ball* of *hammered iron;* it had been fashioned as nearly round as practicable, evidently by the hammer; this ball is still in Col. Davenport's possession. Query, who were the persons who manufactured this ball, and how was it brought to the banks of the Peketonica?

are to be found immense districts of fertile prairie and meadow, why is it that no vestige or remains of a material so indestructible as charred wood, have been discovered? Not in the very numerous diggings throughout the mineral region; not in the various cultivations of the farmer, can any evidence be found of the *roots of trees;* not even the fibre of a root throughout the vast prairies! How is this? The fact deserves not only to be borne in mind by all writers, in investigating the early history of Wisconsin, but it appears to me a conclusive proof that the prairies were never covered with forest. It is true that the annual conflagrations of the high and dry grass, sweeping over whole districts of prairie and natural meadow, will of course prevent the *spontaneous* growth of young timber; it is also equally true from *present* experience, that wherever the fire is kept out of the prairies, a young growth of hazel and ash commences immediately, and oak and cherry soon make their appearance. But this circumstance only establishes the fact, that the burning of the prairies *keeps down* the growth of timber; it does not prove that the prairies were once covered with wood. I repeat, that the total absence in the prairies of *roots of trees*, and of any pieces of *charred wood*, must lead to the conclusion which I have thus drawn.

A remarkable feature in this district is, that no *swamp*, or accumulation of stagnant water in low places, is to be found of any extent; indeed I know of none which can be called *swamp*. The prairie is always undulating, not level; the springs rise on the high grounds, as well as at the points of hills, and in the meadows; the character of the country for throwing the *water off*, is not only of the first importance with regard to health, but also of the highest recommendation to the agriculturist. In such a country *miasma* must be almost unknown, and in consequence, a host of disorders to which the inhabitants of the less favoured eastern and southern states are subject, are here only known by name. Dr. Smith in his enquiries does not find that the professional services of a physician are often required in this part of the Territory. This fact, of itself, even if it were not coupled with the generally acknowledged truth that inhabitants of cold and dry northern regions are of longer life than other people, would speak volumes of recommendations for the settlement of Wisconsin; health is of the greatest value to the settler in a new country, and here indeed health is to be found.*

* Since the above observations were written, I received the following letter from Dr. A. Hays of Pittsburg, a gentleman well acquainted with the Mississippi country; its insertion here requires no apology.

February 1, 1838.
My dear Sir:
In our conversation yesterday on the subject of the Upper Mississippi you expressed a wish that I should give you my

This country is well deserving of an immediate influx of emigrants, and it is fast filling up. Nine years since, the foot of the white man had scarcely penetrated beyond the state line of Illinois; five years since, the Indian depredations aroused the brave and hardy pioneers of the lead region of Wisconsin, and a band of volunteers, under the command of Col. Henry Dodge, took the field in defence of their new homes, their families, and their hearths! The Black Hawk war was prosecuted, and finished

views respecting the health of that delightful region. My own observation and enquiries justify me in speaking in the most positive terms in favour of its general salubrity. It is exempt from most of those diseases produced by summer heats, and miasmata; and, as Lieut. Lee says in his notes on the Iowa Territory, in speaking of its healthfulness, "pulmonary consumption is not known there." I quote from memory, not having his book before me. Of its exemption from that terrible disease, so fatal in many parts of our country, I entertain not a doubt. A highly respectable physician, who has lived in that quarter for sixteen years, assured me that he had not during that period met with a single case of that disease which *originated there*. My impression is, that pulmonary disease always prevails in any country just in proportion to the cold, damp, north-east winds which it is subject to. The beautiful region of the Upper Mississippi rarely ever is visited by winds from that quarter. They usually come from the south-west, west, and north-west, after having passed over a boundless extent of high, dry prairies. It is this which causes the peculiar *dryness* and *elasticity* of the atmosphere so favourable to health and cheerfulness as I believe.

With best wishes, I am yours,

Gen. Smith.   A. HAYS.

after the victory of Bad Axe. No body of men in any country ever behaved with more bravery than did the mounted volunteers of Wisconsin, the *miners*, as they may with truth be called. They were commanded by a brave spirit, by one whose experience in Indian warfare, and in Indian character, deservedly gave him claim to the distinguished station of their leader. His conduct gained him the applause of his country, and his services in the regular army for some years afterwards, during which time he executed some arduous and important expeditions amongst the Indian bands at the foot of the Rocky Mountains, were highly beneficial to the interests of the general government. It would have been contrary to the feelings of brave and generous citizens if they did not give their full approbation to the act of President Jackson which made Henry Dodge Governor of Wisconsin Territory; his *civil* life has justified the appointment.

I have said that all this has happened within nine years, and now towns are springing up every where; cultivation is advancing with a sure progressive step; the mineral wealth of the country is being brought effectually into operation; rail-roads and canals are in projection, and companies to form them have been incorporated; banks have been established, but these may do more harm than good, in encouraging speculation; colleges and schools are in their infancy as yet, but the citizens of such a country as this cannot be long without the best instruction for their children. A University has been by law established at Belmont, and the public spirit of the citizens of the Territory in all their acts is highly praiseworthy. To close my remarks on the rapid progress of settlement and cultivation of this, so late, Indian country, I saw in the month of September 1837, at Mineral Point, to my utter surprise, one morning, huge bills pasted on the tavern houses, announcing the arrival of a troop of circus riders and a travelling menagerie! The caravans arrived, and during a three days carnival, the eyes of the good citizens of the neighbouring country were feasted with the goodly exhibitions of the enterprising eastern travellers, and I asked myself in astonishment, am I in Wisconsin!

Thus much in general with regard to the Wisconsin land district. I will endeavour briefly, to give you an outline of some distinct parts which I think worthy of notice. I shall confine my observations to the eastern side of the river Mississippi, not because I think this district possesses more or greater advantages than Iowa, or the district west of the river, but as I did not travel in that part of the Territory, and as a little work of merit, written by Lieutenant Lee, has already made the public acquainted with its general features, I forbear to say more than that I am aware of its vast importance, of its richness in woods, waters, fertile lands, and mineral wealth; of its populous and thriving towns along the river, and of the spirit of enterprise in the interior; of the great trade already carried on by the citizens, and the unparalleled increase of population there within one year. All these are known to me to be true, and as the surveys of this part of the country are now being completed, I suppose the lands will come into market in the course of a year; therefore, as its population one year since was only about twelve thousand, and now is about twenty-five thousand, I have no doubt that an application will be made to Congress very soon for erecting that district into a new territory, and I wish it all success.*

* The following paragraph is copied from the Wisconsin Territorial Gazette, printed at Burlington, the present seat of government, and illustrates the present and growing prosperity of the country.

"We have before remarked, substantially, and we now repeat, that there is no other portion of the United States that has suffered so little from the 'pressure of the times' as Wisconsin Territory—we mean western Wisconsin particularly—of the eastern part we cannot speak with certainty, but of the 'west side' we can from close observation and personal knowledge. The truth then is, that we have scarcely felt the pressure; we have, it is true, heard much of it; it has been wrung in our ears from abroad, but our sufferings, (if they deserve the name,) have been 'most in apprehension' or sympathetic in their character. The wild spirit of speculation which raged here a year and more ago, has, it is true, been checked, (and so much the better for that,) but the ordinary and regular routine of business has been conducted pretty much as usual. There have been no mercantile failures which could, properly, be attributed to the times; no stoppages of payment; no curtailment of business; no relaxation of industry; no pretermission of enterprise; and, in a word, very little, of any thing real, to interrupt in a degree worthy of complaint or notice, our steady onward march to prosperity and greatness. We have not, too, as many have, been cursed with that bastard trash, the pretended representative of money, commonly denominated 'shin-plasters.' Bank notes, for the most part, of good and solvent banks, have not been wanting for the ordinary transactions of business; while silver change, dollars, and half dollars, have been abundant enough for all purposes. A Benton mint drop, too, has occasionally been circulated among us. Thus, while the old, and rich, and populous states have been agonizing under the pressure of the times, we have been so far from it as to forbid a murmur of complaint. While a silver dollar cannot be seen at the east in the interval of a month, and then only exhibited as a 'cure for sore eyes' as the saying has it, here its jingle may constantly be heard upon the counters of our merchants and in the purses and pockets of our citizens. Our crops, which were abundant, and of the best quality, awarded fair cash prices; and indeed, so far as we are concerned ourselves, were it not for the murmurings of complaint from abroad, which will always meet with a sympathetic response from generous bosoms, we should hardly know that there was any distress existing in the land.

PRAIRIE DU CHIEN.

Pike's-hill—Mouth of Wisconsin—Prairie—Cordon on the Bluffs—Height of the River—Pére Hennepin's Travels—Fort Crevecœur—Checagou—Query—Fort Crawford—New Town—Court-house—Rev. D. Lowry—Congregation—Early Settlers—Half Breeds—Old Town—Old Fort of Prairie du Chien—American Fur Company's Warehouse—Farms of the Old Settlers—Soil and Productions—New City—Importance—Bluffs—Limit of Territory—Hospitality.

AFTER passing Pike's-hill on the west, and the mouth of the Wisconsin river on the east side of the Mississippi, a wide stretch of prairie opens on the left bank of the river; this prairie is skirted and bounded on the east and south-east by a range of high bluffs and rocky hills, surmounted with a growth of low and scattered wood, and the *cordon* occasioned by the washings of the river, appearing high on the face of the bluffs and rocks, and extending up the river gives full evidence that the Mississippi was at one time hemmed in by these bluffs, and consequently that the prairie was once the bed of the river. The plain here is about two miles wide from the river to the bluffs, and about six miles in extent from north to south. The same *cordon* on the face of the rocky bluffs and hills is apparent as high as the Falls of St. Anthony, or as father Hennepin in his travels calls them, the Falls of Saint Anthony of Padua. I suppose from observation, without means of measurement, that at the time the river caused the marked line along the rocky facings of the now distant banks, it must have flowed at least one hundred and fifty feet, if not more, above its present level! What an extensive field of theory, hypothesis and conjecture is here opened, in relation to the waters, the lakes, the prairies, the natural meadows, and the fertility of soil of this interesting country.

Having alluded to Pére Hennepin, and adverting to his book from memory alone, I think that he says he was taken prisoner, above Prairie du Chien, in 1680, or about that time, by the Indians, and carried up the river above the Falls of St. Anthony; when liberated, and being on his return to Quebec, he ascended the Wisconsin river in a canoe; that he arrived at a point on the river whence there was a short portage across low and swampy ground, to the waters of a river which descended into the great Bay des Puants,* part of Illinois lake. This point is where Fort Winnebago now stands, and the portage is not more than a mile and a half over to

---

* Now called "Green Bay."

the Fox river; of this connection I will speak hereafter. One word further on the subject of Hennepin's travels; I recollect that he also says, his party about 1680, and before the unfortunate death of La Salle, being in some distress, built a fort on the Illinois river, which they named in their own language "Crevecœur," or sad heart; as we would say, Fort Distress. The Indians, he observes, called this place "Checagou." The fort was built four days journey *down* the river, from the great town of Illinois. Now, the query is whether in the neighbourhood of the present town of Peoria, near which place, according to the old maps, Crevecœur was situated, there are any remains of the old French fort; it is worthy of enquiry. Perhaps Hennepin's work might be consulted with advantage, now, respecting the state of the country one hundred and fifty years ago; I know not if the book can be obtained, except in public libraries.

To return from this digression, to Prairie du Chien; approaching the town the first object that commands our attention is Fort Crawford, with its noble quadrangular range of buildings, and the military hospital with its excellent garden, in its neighbourhood. This military post or depot stands on an elevated mound in the prairie, about a quarter of a mile from the river, there being a gradual and gentle ascent from the beach to the esplanade in front of the fort. The post may be properly considered as a barrack or depot for arms and munitions of war, and provisions, rather than as a fort of aggression or defence. At the angles of the quadrangle, large open spaces have been left, by erecting four *detached* buildings on the sides of the square, and this place might be rendered a most efficient post of defence against Indian warfare, by the erection of four salient block houses, with embrasures, and thus connecting the whole of the buildings; but at this day, *in this quarter*, Indian aggression is not to be feared.

A short distance north of the fort, the buildings of the new town of Prairie du Chien, or Saint Friole, commence. There are three or four stores in the town, and several excellent private dwellings built on two parallel streets, amongst which are the houses of General Joseph M. Street, the Indian Agent, Judge Lockwood and others; and at the Temperance Hotel of Mr. Tainter, the traveller will forget his locality so far in the western wilds, in the excellent entertainment which he will here receive. The town extends a considerable distance up the prairie, the houses being widely separated. A new stone court-house and public offices have lately been finished, and I may now remark, that during my stay here, I was much pleased and instructed in attending divine service on the Sabbath day, in the court-house, and in listening to an excellent discourse delivered by the Rev. D. Lowry who is stationed in this neighbourhood, and is teacher of a Winnebago school; he is a gentleman of strong mind and of original conceptions, eloquent and persuasive. The numerous congregation, their perfect decorum, and the presence of so many well dressed ladies and gentlemen, formed a powerful and striking contrast with the rude and half naked Indians who were within a stone's cast of the preacher.

About a mile and a half above the new town is a small village inhabited by the descendants of the old French settlers; several of these are *half breeds*, as the early settlers intermarried with Indian women; a slough, *slue*, or arm of the Mississippi called "Marais de St. Friole," separates the new town, or St. Friole, from the old fort and village of Prairie du Chien. The distance across the slough and over the intervening meadow land, to the bank of the Mississippi, on which the old town, and the warehouse of the American Fur Company is built, is about a mile. Here also stood the old fort of Prairie du Chien, now in ruins, nothing being left but the remains of the magazine, and some ranges of decayed barracks. The company's warehouse is a fine three story stone building, about sixty feet square; here is always a great stock of merchandise suitable for the Indian market, not only exposed to sale in the spacious store which occupies nearly the whole of the ground floor, but much of the merchandise is in boxes and packages ready for transportation to other stations where the company has stores and trading houses. This place is also a depot for the furs and articles of trade delivered by the Indians to the traders and agents of the company at different times and places, and here collected until sent down the river to the general depot at St. Louis. This station is under the direction of Mr. Hercules L. Dousman, with whom I passed an agreeable hour.

The houses of the old French settlers, are stretched along the bank of the river, and their little farms are on the prairie back of the new town, and of Fort Crawford. These farms are laid out with narrow fronts on the river, and extend back to the bluffs and hills skirting the prairie. The soil is loose and sandy, yet sufficiently rich to produce excellent crops every year without manuring. Wheat, barley, oats, beans, peas, potatoes, turnips, and all garden vegetables are here most plentifully raised. I am informed by a gentleman who resides here, and has done so for thirty years past, that in all his time, there has been no manure put on this prairie by the old settlers, and that the ground is always ploughed the same way, owing to the narrow fronts and deep extent of the lots from the river; and that the same crops are generally put in every year; and even with this sort of cultivation the yield is superior to any he had known in the eastern states.

About half a mile south of Fort Crawford, a new *city* of Prairie du Chien has been laid out in lots; one or two small frame buildings are now being put up. This situation on the Prairie and on the bank of the Mississippi, at the only place where a good and convenient ferry landing can be had for a considerable distance above and below, is certainly an eligible site for a large town, which, in the regular course of the progressive improvement of the country, must surely in time become a highly important and populous place. Although it is laid out more than two miles above the mouth of the Wisconsin river, yet as there is no proper spot at the mouth for erecting a city upon, owing to the level lowness of the ground, which is not only cut up with bayous and sloughs, but is also subject to overflowings of the two rivers, the town must succeed. The immense trade, particularly in lumber from the upper Mississippi, and of the whole of the Wisconsin river, from its source to its entrance into the Mississippi, must naturally designate Prairie du Chien as a point where a future traveller will find a populous mercantile city, surrounded by a highly cultivated country, and possessing a trade whose extent it would be difficult now, to anticipate or determine.

On the bluffs east of the town of Saint Friole, or new town of Prairie du Chien are some remarkable white sand-stone rocks, as purely white as refined loaf sugar, and of sparkling brilliancy; the stone pulverizes with ease; these bluffs are covered with straggling timber, and intersected by deep ravines; the high lands continue in the same character for some distance to the eastward, into the Indian country. The territory of the United States around Prairie du Chien is very limited, as it lies in the north-western extremity of the purchases, on the east side of the Mississippi.

This place cannot be left by me without speaking of the hospitality of its inhabitants; if cordiality of reception, refined society, and luxuries of the table in eating and drinking, can efface from the mind of the traveller the thought that he is here on the verge of the white settlements, such thought will be lost in the houses of the citizens of the town, and in the apartments of the officers of the garrison. I always shall remember with much pleasure the few days I passed at Prairie du Chien.

THE MILITARY ROAD.

Brunet's Ferry—Wisconsin River—Steamboat Science—Towns on the River, Sutherland, Buchanan—Blue River—La Fayette—River Trade—Brooklyn—Natural Meadows—Beautiful Scenery—Woods—Great Prairie—Hincklin's—Rich Country—Parish's—Lead Diggings—New Furnace—Fine Farm—Wingville—Pedlar's Creek Diggings—Groceries—Diamond Grove—Terry's—Bequette's—Road to Mineral Point—Dodgeville—Governor's Residence—Great Road—Farms on the Prairie—Messersmith's—Numerous Farms—Blue Mounds—Brigham's—Splendid view—Moundville—Old Fort—Grave of Lieut. Force—Interesting Anecdote.

LEAVING the Prairie, the military road to Fort Winnebago, which has been laid out within a few years, passes through a cultivated country for about six miles, where it strikes the Wisconsin river at the highly improved farm of Mr. Jean Brunet; here is an excellent large stone house and well finished barn with many other convenient buildings; Mr. Brunet resides at the Prairie, but attends to the cultivation of the farm personally. The river is here crossed in a ferry boat, and is between four and five hundred yards broad; it is navigable for steamboats from its mouth to Fort Winnebago; the only boat which *regularly* plies on the river, is the Science, Captain Clark, commander, whose first voyage was made in June last, and much credit is due to his enterprise in attempting, and succeeding in the difficult navigation of the Wisconsin. This river is thickly studded with wooded islands, and the true channel is difficult to find owing to the peculiar character of its sandy bottom, which occasions numerous bars and shoals; and yet this noble river, notwithstanding such obstacles, will doubtless on sufficient examination be rendered as safe in its channels for steamboat navigation as the Ohio; the difficulties of navigation decrease with each voyage that is made. The first time that the Science descended the river, your townsman Dr. Joel B. Sutherland was a passenger; he informs me, they descended with great facility, and that several islands, bluffs and points were then baptized, which may in all probability hereafter retain the names then given to them. Several towns have been laid out on the southern side of the river, the northern side is still Indian country. Some of these towns have highly eligible locations, particularly one, laid out by a number of gentlemen in the Territory, who own the property, at Prairie du Bay, opposite the mouth of the Kickapoo river, called "Sutherland;" this site has an excellent steamboat *landing*, and they are not numerous on the river; one nearly opposite Pine river and Long Island called "Buchanan;" from this town, which is at the mouth of Mineral creek, there is a proposed rail-road to Dodgeville, passing through a mineral region, and thus giving the means of transportation of heavy material to water carriage on the Wisconsin. Savannah, English Prairie, Helena, Arena, St. Lawrence, Winnebago city, and many other towns are laid out on the river. Some of the best lead diggings in the Territory are found on Blue river, which empties into the Wisconsin about twenty miles above Brunet's Ferry; and at the forks of Blue river a few miles above its mouth, a town is laid out, called La Fayette. The trade on the river will certainly foster the incipient existence of these towns, and in a few years, we shall see the wooded banks of the Wisconsin giving place to the active bustle of farming, manufacturing and business of all description.

After crossing the river at Brunet's ferry, the road passes for a mile or two, over very low and swampy ground; a town has also been laid out here called "Brooklyn," but its site is not favourable, being too low. Passing over the low ground, the military road enters a wide ravine of natural meadow, through which meanders a considerable stream of pure spring water, in which are abundance of trout. At various places the natural meadow extends on both sides of the road, in little coves between the hills which bound the meadow, forming delightful fertile spots of twenty or thirty acres, connected of course with the main meadow; at the head of these divergings, are seen small groves of timber, and the dwarf willow, which invariably indicates the presence of the limpid spring: above, and surrounding the whole scene, are the wood-crowned hills, and altogether this part of the country presents many delightful spots for the farmer, the grazier, and the country gentleman, who is fond of beautiful scenery.

About six miles from the river the road ascends the hills and passes through a tolerably well wooded country for about five miles more, when it emerges into the extensive, rich upland prairie, extending for near seventy miles eastward to the Four Lake country, and southward to the Platte mounds; in fact the great prairie of the Wisconsin land district. Travellers are much indebted to the kindness of Mr. Hincklin, who resides here, on the verge of the prairie, for the accommodations which his establishment affords to the weary way-farer. He has a good farm, some seventy or eighty acres in wheat, corn, oats and potatoes; the soil of the first quality; this place is about twenty miles north-east from Cassville on the Mississippi; several settlements are in this neighbourhood, and here is an excellent location for a house of entertainment for travellers, as this military road will always be a leading one through the territory.

From the farm of Mr. Hincklin, the road continues through a most luxuriant rolling prairie, intersected with fine groves and strips of timber, and at the distance of about forty miles from Prairie du Chien, the fine farm and smelting-furnace of Thomas I. Parish, Esq. greets the view. Between Hincklin's and Parish's farms, several most desirable farming sites are found, and the whole country is abundantly rich in soil, and well supplied with timber. About half way, there are some old cabins, and an improvement; this place was an encampment of Governor Dodge during the Black Hawk war, and here are found several fine springs of water, and much excellent timber.

At the farm of Mr. Parish, we are in the immediate vicinity of the mineral region: the Blue river diggings are in this neighbourhood, and those of Mr. Parish are amongst the most productive in the territory. He has lately erected a new smelting-furnace on a new principle, termed *reverberating;* the mineral is enclosed in an oven, on an inclined plane, and the heat by the proper application of the blast, is carried over and around the *galena*, and the advantages over the common smelting-furnace are said to be very great, in the saving of fuel, and the rapidity and extent of the *yield* of the ore.

The improvements of Mr. Parish are extensive. He has in all his entries more than 1600 acres of prairie and woodland; his buildings are good and commodious; his farm well cultivated, his product abundant, and his kindness and hospitality to travellers well known. Besides the fine springs near his dwelling-house, a number of pure fountains break out from the sides of the hill near his furnace, and uniting in a dell below his furnace, fall over a ledge of rocks about sixteen feet, and give him an excellent and never failing water power; this is one of the heads of Blue river. Fine limestone is abundant here, and also blocks of building stone, easily dressed, and equal to the best material in the east. Mr. Parish has been settled here since the year 1828. There is a Post office established here called "Wingville."

A few miles east of Wingville a road diverges from the main military road, and passing to the south-east, leads through a mineral region called Pedlar's creek diggings, or Cahoe's diggings; here are a number of buildings called "Groceries," establishments for the *comfort* and *entertainment* of the miners; this road leads also through the fine body of wood called "Diamond Grove" to Mineral Point. In the grove are the old furnace of Mr. Terry, and the excellent new establishment of Col. Bequette, a son-in-law of Governor Dodge, consisting of dwellings, store, farm, and smelting-furnace.

From Col. Bequette's the country becomes hilly and rough, covered with hazle bushes, but still the soil is excellent. Powell's large smelting-furnace is on the Peketonica, which is crossed about two miles from Diamond Grove, and two miles from the crossing, stands the town of Mineral Point; of this place more shall be said hereafter, let us return to the Military road and pursue our way to the Four lake country.

From Parish's the road continues through the rich prairie, with here and there on its verge the new settlements and improvements springing up, until the traveller arrives in sight of Dodgeville, about a mile south of the road. This is a small collection of habitations of the miners, at which is established the store and farm of Henry L. Dodge and Augustus C. Dodge. The mineral diggings in this neighbourhood are numerous and valuable, and they are amongst the first which were worked in the country. The residence of the Governor is two or three miles south of Dodgeville, on the road to Mineral Point, and is situated in the bosom of a thick grove, surrounded by lofty timber for a mile and more on all sides except the south-east, which opens on the rich prairie a few hundred yards from the dwelling-house, and here are the cultivated fields and the luxuriant garden of the proprietor. At this place is a smelting furnace, carried on by the sons of the Governor; a new cupola furnace is now being erected on a new plan of smelting ore, and the excellent quality of the building stone, together with the firm and neat style of the building itself, renders this establishment inferior to none in the country; the cupola stack has the appearance from a distance, of a towering obelisk, seen through the openings of the grove.

Fine springs of pure water abound here, and the residence of Governor Dodge may be considered as a selection of great judgment amidst so many fine locations around him. In the company of his amiable family, and in the friendly hospitalities of his mansion, I passed many hours.

The great road from Galena, through Mineral Point and Dodgeville to Helena on the Wisconsin river, intersects the Military road near the Dodgeville diggings; from this point several interesting new settlements are seen on the prairie, and these farms increase on each side of the road, until the traveller reaches the Blue mounds; from this latter place to Madison at the Four lakes, a distance of about twenty miles, the country is yet unsettled, although perhaps as good a farming district as any in the Territory, and possessing the advantages of lying along the great leading road across the country, from the Mississippi to the lake; a road that must always continue at or near its present location, as it has been judiciously laid out, from Prairie du Chien to Fort Winnebago, along a ridge which divides the waters of the Wisconsin from those of the Peketonica and the heads of Rock river, and it traverses a rich arable prairie for near one hundred miles.

Amongst the fine farms in this section, is that of Mr. John Messersmith, a Pennsylvanian, from Franklin county; he is one of the earliest settlers in the Territory, and like all the pioneers, commenced with his lead diggings. His farm is in the best cultivation; his crops abundant; a more beautiful sight I never witnessed on any farm in Pennsylvania, than the very numerous shocks of wheat and oats in his grain-fields, and the promise of a plentiful crop of corn, potatoes and ruta baga. His mines are productive, and in addition to lead and copper, and the prospects of a valuable iron mine on his land, his advantages of wood, natural meadow, fine springs of water, plenty of lime stone, and excellent mill powers on Pipe run, all render the farm and lands of Messer Grove amongst the most eligible for a capitalist of any in the country.

Dr. Smith and myself spent a week at this place, making our daily excursions in the vicinity, in company with the proprietor in one of his carriages; and as he is intimately acquainted with the whole country, and there is no difficulty of traversing the prairies and groves in any direction, I derived much information, from personal view, and from the experience of Mr. Messersmith. I should be wanting in justice were I not to mention the agreeable society I found in his family; he has raised several sons and daughters whose respectable station in the world must gratify the parents; one of his sons is Probate Judge of Iowa county.

Twelve miles from this farm, the Blue mounds, the great land marks, or as I am told Dr. Sutherland designates them, *day-light beacons,* rise in towering grandeur, covered by dense wood to the summit; these hills are two in number, and are seen from all parts of the district. Between Messer Grove and the Blue mounds, the farms are numerous and in excellent cultivation; at the mounds resides Col. Brigham, a member of the council, who has mineral advantages on his locations, particularly *carbonate* of lead, which is found here, in addition to *sulphurate* or *galena*. He also has large bodies of fine timber, extensive prairie, part of the mound, and the most splendid situation for a residence that the lover of the beauties of natural scenery could desire. On the side of the mound, about one hundred feet above the prairie, with a gentle ascent to the location from the plain below, rise several pure springs of delightful water; here is the dwelling-house; behind and on each side rise the steeps of the Blue mound, covered with hazle bushes and the common trees of the country, interspersed with various fruits and vines indigenous to the soil; in front, to the south, the eye takes in at a view an extent of forty or fifty miles of the most interesting country. Undulating prairie, covered with flowers, and studded with beautiful groves and groups of timber, and streams of purest water intersecting and pervading the whole; such a view as is seen from the Platte mounds at Belmont, and these mounds appear in the south-west, distance about forty-five miles, rising on the horizon as the *rival beacons* of their brethren here. When the country at the foot, and lying south of the Blue mounds becomes settled, and villages have sprung up over the vast extent of cultivatable land, which the eye here grasps at a glance, the day will arrive when future thousands will flock on excursions of pleasure to the Blue mounds: mineral springs are found here, on and around the mounds, their qualities not yet ascertained.

A post office is established here, called "Moundville;" there are two hills or mounds, from two to three hundred feet above the plain; there is a good farm at the foot of the western mound, the establishment of Mr. Kellog, at which travellers find an excellent resting place, and the very fine improvements of Col. Brigham are on, and at the foot of, the eastern mound; around and on the summit of this monnd I am informed, that more than one thousand acres of excellent arable land is found, and water also is there; at the foot of the mounds, and about a quarter of a mile from the road, stands the old Mound Fort, consisting of two block-houses and a picket fence; during the Black Hawk war several families were forted and protected here for a time; Lieut. Force was killed by the Indians in front of the fort, and his grave is now seen close to the road side, and near the spot where he was shot; the Indians were in ambush in the grass in a small ravine, and the whole scene was visible from the fort, which is about half a mile west of the place. A sortie was made, but the Indians escaped, and the one that killed Lieut. Force, robbed him of his gold watch and chain; this Indian was afterwards shot at the Four lakes in a skirmish between the savages and Col. Dodge's volunteers; I have understood that Dr. A. Philleo of Galena was the person who killed him; the body of the Indian was left where he fell, unexamined; and some months afterwards, Col. Brigham of the Blue mounds, passing by the dead body, over which, in the mean time, a prairie fire had passed, and consumed the remnants of the Indian's clothing, picked up his pouch, in which was found the watch and chain of the unfortunate Force; these were subsequently restored to his family.

THE FOUR LAKES.

Numerous Mounds—Fine Prairie—Large body of Wood—River of the Four Lakes—City of Madison—The Fourth Lake—Catfish River—Beauty of the Fourth Lake—Fish—Stones—Seat of Government—Extension of the City—Various names—Rapid progress—Public Buildings—Canal—First Lake—Question as to Location of Seat of Government—Additions to Madison—Public Improvements—City of the Four Lakes—Canal to Wisconsin river—Illinois Improvements in Rock river—Great Advantages of Situation—Superb Scenery—Stage Coach—Fort Winnebago—Canal—Portage—Communication with the Atlantic—Happy tendency to Union.

From the Blue mounds the road passes through alternate prairie and wood, crossing one of the head waters of Sugar river, until within eight miles of the Four lakes, where the traveller leaves the Military road, which trends to the north-east, immediately after emerging from a considerable tract of oak openings, and again entering the prairie. Along this part of the road the mounds or burial places are numerous, and a short distance north of the road, immediately after crossing the Sugar river waters, the spot which I have before described as being similar to a ploughed field, is situated, under a high ledge of rocky hills, and adjoining two very long parallel Indian mounds: I am particular in this description of locality, in order to direct attention to the place, as worthy of examination.

Leaving the main road, and travelling eastward over the rolling prairie, which is susceptible of the highest cultivation, although immediately on the track there is a scarcity of wood, in about four miles ride, you enter a fine body of timber, which continues without interruption of prairie for four miles further, when the fourth and the third lakes burst on the astonished view, in all their splendid watery and picturesque grandeur.

The river of the Four Lakes is one of the principal streams forming Rock river of Illinois; with slight improvements in the navigation, boats may pass from the Mississippi for at least three hundred miles, up Rock river, and the Four Lake river to the city of Madison, the present established seat of government of Wisconsin. This city is laid out on a narrow strip of land lying between the fourth and the third lake; the elevated ground near the centre of the city on which the government buildings are now being erected, commands a fine view over both lakes, and of course over the surrounding parts of the contemplated city.

The fourth lake is a beautiful sheet of water, six miles from east to west, and four miles from north to south, in its widest parts; its regular circumference being interrupted by the protrusion of wooded points of land into the lakes. The water is from fifty to seventy feet deep, and always preserves its pure clearness, and sea-like appearance in colour, although sometimes disturbed into a considerable tumult of waves by high winds. The third lake is less than the fourth, and the second and first lakes gradually diminish in size until the river of the Four Lakes continues its regular course to the junction with Rock river. These lakes are of course connected by a continuous channel or outlet from one lake to the other, which channel is sometimes called *Catfish* river, but is properly the Four Lake river, or river of the Four Lakes, and is so designated in all the old maps of this country. I do not know that there is any water power on this connecting channel.

Springs arise all around these lakes, particularly the fourth lake, supplying the great mass of waters; but a principal source is a considerable stream of two or three branches, emptying in, on the northern shore of the fourth lake; no situation can be conceived more beautiful than the shores of this lake; the land rises gently all around its margin, receding and rising gradually into a gentle eminence, for about a mile from the lake, and the whole of this lovely shore is studded and adorned with spots of wood and thick groves, giving the idea of the park scenery in England, or the rich views of Italy; and more beautiful than either, in its natural state. The lake abounds with the finest fish, perch, bass, catfish, buffalo fish, muskelonge, from a pound weight to thirty pounds and more. The shores are lined with fine shingle and white sand, and amongst the pebbles are found chalcydone, agate, and cornelian, and other fine and beautiful stones suitable for seals, breast-pins, and other ornaments, not only often but in abundance.

Although the seat of government, "Madison," is laid out on the strip of land between the lakes, and the public buildings are located here, yet an extension of city lots has been made by the land proprietors all around the fourth lake; the different sites bear the names of East Madison, North Madison, the City of the Four Lakes, and Mandamus. I have called Madison a contemplated city: let it be remembered that six months since, the site of the city was government land, unlocated and in a state of nature; now there are about thirty houses in a state of forwardness; a steam saw-mill nearly completed;* a population of above one hundred active mechanics and labourers employed in their own improvements, and in the erection of the public buildings, which are already in a forward state, the stone foundations being up to the surface of the ground, and abundance of material already delivered, to keep the work in

* This mill is now (1838) in full operation.

THE FOUR LAKES.

progress, and all matters going on actively: add to this picture of enterprise and industry the excellent accommodations which are obtained at the public house of Mr. Peck, and the traveller may well be surprised at the rapid progress of the city of Madison.

The connection between the fourth and the third lake is not navigable for steamboats at present, the stream is narrow and rapid, and bounds the city of Madison on the east; it is in contemplation to cut a canal through the city, to connect the lakes, which of course will render property on its margin more valuable for business purposes than in other parts of the city; but the most pleasant streets for dwellings and where the trading and business will be carried on for some years, are in the vicinity of the state house and public square. The distance from the head of the fourth lake to the foot of the first lake is about fourteen miles, and on the western bank of this lake is laid out a town called "The City of the First Lake;" I did not visit it, and cannot therefore speak of its localities.

Much excitement existed in the Territory in regard to the act of the Legislature fixing the seat of government at Madison; many rival towns *already* in existence, and many eligible *sites* had their respective claims. It is not for me to form a hasty judgment on the strength of these claims, nor on the propriety of the present location of the seat of government; the principal objection is, the absence of *central position*. A glance at the map will satisfy the observer touching this matter, and the contemplated acquisition of new territory north and west of the Wisconsin river, which eventually will take place, may render this objection stronger; and yet if Iowa Territory is separated, which also may shortly occur, the position in regard to *centrality*, (have I coined a word?) will be in favour of Madison. The country around the lakes is susceptible of high improvement: there is plenty of timber, of limestone, and of the best building material, and certainly agriculturists would do well to settle in this neighbourhood immediately, as an influx of population daily takes place, and the prices of grain and provisions are very high at present; the buildings in the new city are daily increasing, and as Congress has already appropriated twenty thousand dollars to erect the public buildings, I cannot believe that the immediate growth of Madison can be checked, even by the dissatisfaction originally exhibited as to its location as the seat of government.

With regard to the several additions to Madison, laid out around the eastern and northern shores of the fourth lake, the towns may not for some years meet the sanguine expectations of the several proprietors, but it may with truth be said, that in whatever proportion population and business may increase in all or any of these places, compared with other parts of the Territory, there cannot be found in any part of Western Wisconsin situations more healthy, land more fertile, or prospects more beautiful in respect to land and water scenery, than around and in the vicinity of the Four Lakes; this region must in a short time be thickly inhabited.

Many works of great public improvement are in projection with regard to this important section of country. A rail-road is in contemplation, to be made from the city of Mississippi, (which is laid out on the river opposite to Eagle Point, two miles above Dubuque,) by way of the town of Belmont, New Baltimore, Mineral Point, Dodgeville and Moundville, to the city of the Four Lakes, and thence around the fourth lake, north and east by the city of Madison on its eastern boundary, and thence in an east course to Milwaukie. From the city of the Four Lakes there is a road to Fort Winnebago and thence to Green Bay; there is also a road to Milwaukie, and a good road to the Wisconsin river at Arena.

The site of the city of the Four Lakes, *opposite* to Madison on the north side of the lake, is a most beautiful location. Governor Dodge in his first message to the legislature said that the Indians had been known to have passed in canoes from Wisconsin river to the Four Lakes, the distance being only about twelve miles. He therefore thought it a work of but little labour to make a communication between these two points.* It is quite probable that the legislature at its next session will pass a

* The following is an extract from the message of Governor Dodge.

"The improvement of the navigation of Fox river, I consider a subject of great importance to the citizens of this Territory, and recommend that an appropriation be asked of Congress for a survey of the Fox river from Green Bay to Fort Winnebago. A small appropriation would remove the obstructions at the Grand and Little Kakalin, and by cutting a canal a short distance, one third of the distance would be shortened between Lake Winnebago and the portage of the Wisconsin and Fox rivers. A canal, already commenced, of one mile and a quarter, will connect the waters of the Wisconsin and Fox rivers. This important public work has been commenced by an enterprising company, under a charter from the Territory of Michigan, and it is expected will be completed the next season. With the improvement of the navigation of the Fox river, and connecting the waters of the Wisconsin with that river, we would have an internal communication between Lake Michigan and the Mississippi river, which would greatly facilitate our commercial operations on the Lakes, as well as the transportation of troops and munitions of war, should it be necessary, for the protection of our exposed and extensive frontier.

The improvement of the navigation of the Rock river, I consider a subject of vital importance to the future prosperity of this Territory. This river waters a large extent of fertile country; a small appropriation by Congress, would be sufficient to remove the obstructions in its navigation. It is known, that, from the outlet of the four lakes, that discharges itself into the Rock river, the distance does not exceed twelve miles by land, and from the fourth lake, it is not more than sixteen miles to the Wisconsin river. Indians have frequently descended in canoes, in high waters, from the fourth lake to the Wisconsin river. The great advantage of this inland law for that purpose. To add to the further interest of this portion of the country, the State of Illinois has appropriated a large sum of money to improve the navigation of Rock river up to the south line of the Wisconsin Territory. The river of the Four Lakes, sometimes improperly called Catfish river, runs into Rock river; of course by the Illinois improvement, and some assistance from the legislature of Wisconsin, a perfect navigation will soon be effected, when boats in great numbers will be seen ascending Rock river from the Mississippi, through the Four Lakes.*

Indeed I can scarcely say enough in relation to this charming region. The present easy access to this section of country, by ascending the Mississippi to Galena, Mississippi city, Cassville, or Prairie du

communication must be apparent; it would greatly enhance the value of the national domain in that part of the Territory, and increase the value of lands purchased by individuals from the government. The construction of a rail-road, commencing at some suitable point on the Mississippi, in this Territory, passing through the mining country to the Rock river, and direct to lake Michigan, is a subject of great interest to the citizens of this Territory, who have strong claims on the patronage of the Government in granting a donation in land for that important purpose.

* The Wisconsin Legislature has during its present Session created a company to connect Rock river with Milwaukie river, which empties into Lake Michigan at the growing town of Milwaukie. (1838.)

Chien, and thence over the delightful prairies to the Four Lakes will undoubtedly make it the frequent summer resort of the southern planters. Surrounded as it is with the purest air, and a most healthful climate, not surpassed, if equalled, in any of the old States, visiters here can never fail to enjoy themselves either in admiring its picturesque scenery, or by bathing or fishing in these crystal lakes, in which are to be found most delicious varieties of the finny tribe.

In my judgment no American gentleman should visit Europe until he had made the grand western tour. There are *single* points, for instance the Platte mounds, Helena, the Blue mounds, and the place I have been describing, in our own beautiful and fertile west, worth all the time and expense consumed in the journey from the borders of the Atlantic, to the *recent* home of the roaming Indians: great numbers of foreigners traverse these prairies and woodland grounds of enchantment every year.*

---

* The following is an extract from a letter published in July 1837, in the National Intelligencer, relative to this part of Wisconsin; the writer is generally understood to be G. W. Featherstonehaugh, Esq.

"Beyond Galena, on the way to the Four Lakes, are two or three respectable farmers, well to do in the world, who attend to mining at their leisure moments; they began the world as miners, and have become farmers. Mr. Messersmith is one of these; his wife and daughters are active in every hospitable attention, and are quite agreeable women; the master of

A stage coach departs once a week to and from Galena and Fort Winnebago, and is generally well

the house has reared a large family of sons and daughters, and, on account of his being one of the oldest settlers in the country, and one of the most intelligent men in the territory, has a good deal of influence there. Besides entertaining me with amusing narratives of his early adventures with the Indians, he laid me under real obligations to his hospitality. About fifteen miles from his pretty situation, chosen on account of a charming spring, are the Blue mounds, extensive elevations or outliers, seen from a great distance on the prairie. From these mounds to the Four Lakes the distance is about 22 miles. As soon as you leave the military road which leads to Fort Winnebago, the country, which is always singularly fertile, begins to grow more wooded, and at about eight miles assumes a character of the most winning beauty. The rolling bald prairie changes not to an abruptly broken country, but the ridges here are all resolved into masses of gracefully rounded hills, constantly separated by gentle depressions, often becoming deepened valleys, through which some of the heads of Sugar river, a tributary of Rock river, take their course. In whatever direction your eyes turn, these irregularities of surface present themselves; but that which imparts an indescribable charm to the whole scene, from the knoll where you stand to where these alternate hills and vales blend with the horizon, is the inimitable grace with which the forests and clumps of trees are disposed. Here a grove upon the slope of a hill, distinguished by its richness and symmetry from its numerous companions, impends over the amenity of the rich valley beneath, whilst further on a more robust line of dense foliage betrays the ampler volume of the pellucid stream which nourishes it. Every part within the range of the horizon is alike, in that each, turn where you will, concurs to cherish and render more indelible the new and pleasing impression, whilst the parts separately, having each a softness of character contrasted occasionally with the filled with passengers. Fort Winnebago is at the present head of navigation on the Wisconsin river,

noble escarpments that peer out from the bluffs at the very moment when you are ready to say that Nature has exceeded the finest style of English park scenery, tell you in terms that must be listened to, that you have never seen any thing so beautiful, so really attractive, before, and that it is a pure American scene, the elements of which no magic could enable all Europe to bring together. Beneath your feet is an ancient Indian trail, steadily holding its course betwixt the waters of the *Mississippi* and the *Tychoaberah*. It is always safe to follow that. Along this trail my two intelligent companions and myself discovered Indian monuments of a remarkable character, the figures of men raised from four to six feet in alto relievo from the sod, head arms, body, and legs, perfectly distinct, and about 120 feet long. At one point was a figure of this kind with seven buffaloes or *animal mounds* evidently intended for them; head with horns, fore and hind legs, back and tail, also about 40 yards long, all in a line succeeding to each other. Where these groups were, was generally a round mound, probably the depository of the body of the chief, some great buffalo hunter, in whose honour these monuments were raised. We always found these on the line of the trail, or not far from them.

If the scenery had been insufficient, these were enough to keep up the American feeling, and, if I could have been insensible to that, the occasional glimpse of the shy deer with her beautiful fawn, and the more frequent flushing of the prairie hen from her nest, would have brought me back to it. But no assertions can do justice to the surprising fertility of the soil, capable of raising any thing and every thing susceptible of cultivation with the least degree of expense; cold in the long winter, but dry and salubrious throughout the year, and destined to become a populous and powerful country, despite the frauds and misrepresentations which now bring it into discredit. Who would have thought that brokers, specu-

and a portage of about a mile and a half across a level and low country, connects a line of water communication from Prairie du Chien to Green Bay, and consequently to New York and Pennsylvania. This portage can now be passed in wet seasons, in canoes, from one river to the other,* and thus if a canal were cut through this small space of ground, a traveller might leave New York or Philadelphia, pass round by sea to New Orleans, ascend the Mississippi, and the Wisconsin, and descend Fox river to Green Bay, pass around the Lakes to Erie or Buffalo, and proceed to the Atlantic cities without setting his foot on land. Wonderful country, and how well worthy the continued enterprise of all the friends of those internal improvements, which have the *general* good in view, and whose tendency is to connect *all* our citizens

lators, and sharpers could already have done so much to stigmatize the character of one of the finest domains that Nature ever offered to man."

* I am informed by Judge Irvin of Wisconsin that a company had it in contemplation to cut a canal here—they opened a ditch two feet wide, and the same deep, from one river to the other—the Wisconsin river being higher than the Fox river, the ditch was cut at that end deepest, and when opened, the water flowed freely from river to river.

Schoolcraft says, "Such is the little difference in the level of the two streams, that during high water canoes frequently pass loaded across the lowest parts of the prairie from one to the other."

more closely with each other, by mutual interests, and frequent intercourse, and by such means, to render more indissoluble the bonds of our glorious and happy *Union!*

THE BURIAL MOUNDS.

Form, composition, examination of one; conjectures; no tradition; attempts to account therefor—Pére Lafitau's work—Feast of the Dead—Conjectures—Indian customs—Stone Mounds—Pottery.

These eminences are found in various parts of the Territory—they are very numerous along the track of the Military road from Prairie du Chien to Fort Winnebago—particularly on that part between the Blue mounds and the Four Lakes. They are of various forms or shapes, generally raised from three to five feet above the surrounding prairie, and as far as has been ascertained by digging, the earth of which they are composed is different in colour and consistence from that of the land adjoining and beneath the mounds. It does not require much stretch of imagination to fancy the figure of some of these mounds as approaching that of a buffalo, a snake, a tortoise, and even of a man. Two parallel lines of mounds, near one of the head waters of Sugar river, I measured by stepping, and they were about two hundred and fifty paces in length. On the north shore of the fourth lake, a conical mound, about eight feet high, was opened in my presence, beginning at the summit and digging perpendicularly. At the depth of about five feet we found several pieces of agate arrow heads, some curious pieces of pottery, which had apparently been glazed within and without, and finally came to the skeleton of a human being. We proceeded no further, but my own conjectures were, that more bodies than one had been inhumed there. It was remarkable that there was no adjoining spot whence, apparently, the earth to form the mound could have been taken; such is generally the case with these mounds; they are raised above the surface of the plain, and no neighbouring depression or cavity, whence earth had been removed, appears. The quality of the earth in the mound was of a loose brownish or blackish ashes, with a soapy feel. Can this be the natural decomposition of the human body? and are these mounds common sepultures, or individual graves? most certainly the earth in the neighbourhood is very different; the general quality of the soil near this mound is rich, but slightly mixed with loose small limestone and quartz, yet in the mound, all the earth was as fine and friable as if it had been sifted.

With regard to these mounds it is worthy of remark that the oldest Indian Tribes have no tradition or history relative to them; the present race of Indians inhabiting this part of the country, are totally ignorant of them. In the absence of a written language, of coins, of monuments, and of tradition, there is nothing beyond conjecture, to aid the antiquarian in his researches into the history of the primitive inhabitants of North America. It is true that the ignorance of the present Indians touching these mounds may be accounted for, by the supposition that centuries have elapsed since the tenants of the tomb were deposited here, and the numerous exterminating wars of the several bands that in succeeding times inhabited this country, has totally destroyed even the organs through which tradition might be carried down to us.

Many years since I recollect of reading a French work, entitled "Mœurs des Sauvages Ameriquains comparèes aux Mœurs des premiers Temps, par Pére Lafitau," in which, describing the Great Feast of the Dead, he relates that the Iroquois have a custom at certain intervals of many years, of disinterring all the dead who had been inhumed during the past interval, and each family brings the fragments of remains, the skeletons, the half putrid corpses, and the late dead, of their own kindred, to one general assemblage, and after having been for some days exposed on stages erected for the purpose, during which time the feasting and dancing, and ceremonies in honour of the dead, have their celebration, the numerous remains of the deceased of all ages, who have died within the lapsed period, are gathered into one common depository. This ceremony is renewed at stated periods, the number of years I do not recollect, but this may in a great measure account for the numerous large mounds found in this country and elsewhere on the Mississippi and Ohio. I merely throw out the idea, without arguing on the hypothesis, in the absence of any book of reference.

I cannot forbear remarking that this country may have been inhabited formerly by a nation as powerful and as gifted as the Mexicans were, when Cortez entered their country. I do not place much reliance on the supposed discovery of the city of Aztlan, in the Milwaukee district, although a piece of hardened and burnt clay was shown to me as having been found there, evidently appearing like part of a brick. I look on the city as an assemblage of mounds, and the clay as partaking of the pottery which I discovered in the grave on the fourth lake. And yet it is to be confidently hoped, that as we go forward in exploring and settling this highly interesting country, some vestige may be discovered, some certain and conclusive matter brought to light, on which we may build, not conjectures, but arguments, tending to open up the long buried history of the aborigines of America; a history which no *living* Indian can in any manner elucidate.

In conversing with Judge Irvin of Wisconsin, on the subject of these mounds, he informs me as the result of his enquiries amongst the old and intelligent Indian traders, that the Indians had a custom, on the burial of a chief, or brave, of distinction, to consider his grave as entitled to the tribute of a portion of earth from each passer by. Hence the first grave formed a nucleus, around which, in the accumulation of the daily tributes of respect thus paid, a mound was soon formed, and as the earth was often carried to the grave from some distance, the absence of neighbouring cavities, from which the mound might be raised, may be accounted for. It also became an honourable distinction for other dead to be buried by the side of the chiefs so deposited in the first mound; and as the custom of earthy tribute continued, the mound increased in size, and the present irregularity in the size and shape of the burial places may also thus be explained. The dishonoured dead, and the graves of those who had committed crimes, were stigmatized by the heaping of stones upon them, and the custom of adding a stone, by the traveller, to the unhonoured *cairn* was observed with as much attention as that of heaping the handful of earth on the remains of the chieftain. Hence also the origin of the stone mounds. Compare this custom of the North American Indians in regard to the dead, with the customs of the primitive nations of the eastern hemisphere, and examine Pére Lafitau's "Mœurs des Sauvages," &c.

Pottery is still made by the Indians of the north-west; and brick-making in its rude state, I am informed, has always been, and still is practised by them. These few facts may serve as some data, some slight beginnings on which future investigations may be made, explanatory of the history of the Indian mounds.

HELENA.

Roads—Face of the Country—Splendid Amphitheatre of Meadow—Hay-makers—Feelings of a Traveller—Wisconsin River—United States Store House—Town of Helena—Shot Tower Establishment—New Store House—Description of the Shot Tower—Extensive View—Indian Country.

From Mr. Messersmith's farm to Helena, on the Wisconsin River, the country is well timbered with numerous oak openings, and some miles of thick and well set wood. The distance is about twelve miles, and Mr. Messersmith has at his own expense opened a road for about four miles, until it intersects the main public road from Dodgeville to Helena. The country (after passing over a natural meadow, through which the head waters of Pipe creek run), is hilly, with some remarkable rocky eminences, woody dells, and deep ravines, altogether a romantic country, with abundance of rich land, natural meadow, and fine timber. Four or five miles from Helena the road descends abruptly from the high wooded hills, and one of the most splendid views in the country opens on the traveller. An amphitheatre of meadow, or low prairie, encircled at the point where he enters it, with high and bold hills, and jutting rocks, surmounted with oak openings, lies in broad expanse before him. This meadow is about half a mile wide and about four miles long, to the base of the amphitheatre, along which flows the Wisconsin river. On each side as the road winds through the level plain of verdure, there are deep indentures in the surrounding hills, forming numerous small meadows, or little green coves, interspersed with groups of forest tress, and exhibiting the dwarf willow, the well known companion of the limpid spring. Several small streams unite in the centre of the meadow and form a considerable water-course emptying into the Wisconsin at the northern base of the plain. In looking around on the face of the encircling rocky hills, the fact that this great body of lowland was once the bottom of a lake, or an expansion of the Wisconsin river, appears evident. The action of the water has worn a distinct line on the face of the perpendicular rocks, and the exposed stony face of the hills, and the semblance of a corded line can be traced all around this expanded low prairie, and also around the various extensions and indentations of the little coves amongst the protruding hills and eminences. The meadow land is of the richest alluvial quality. Several persons from Helena were here making hay. They always of course choose the spots where the grass is most tender, and not too tall,—consequently, the great extent of meadow being mowed in various places, and the surrounding hills and little green coves, together with the beautiful natural grouping of the trees, and the delightful springs of pure water pervading the whole, suggest the idea of long settlement and of high cultivation and improvement. The traveller after leaving behind him for many miles immense tracts of wood and uncultivated prairie, feels as if he was transported at once into some happy valley, and surrounded by the residences of a rich population.

Some small enclosed fields near the Wisconsin river give good promise of plentiful crops of corn and potatoes. Not far from the bank of the river is erected a house for a store, near which I observed some Indian graves lately made. Immediately on the bank, a large log building was put up by the United States agent, superintending the lead mines, and was intended as an office and store house for the deposit of the government lead, received from the miners and smelters. From this place it could be readily shipped down the Wisconsin to St. Louis or up the river to Fort Winnebago. The building is going to decay, and I am informed, that all the land in this beautiful valley is *entered* or located, including the government buildings. From this point the road bends abruptly to the east, along the bank of the river, and a ride of two miles or thereabouts through the site of the town of Helena, brings you to the shot tower and buildings belonging to the Wisconsin Shot Company. Here is a large lumber yard, the lumber being chiefly of pine, and brought down the Wisconsin river. Several mechanic's shops are erected, and workmen employed. The Shot Company have a very large assortment of goods and merchandise in their store which is here kept, and on the river bank there is now being built a store house of about fifty by seventy feet, the basement story of stone from the river beach to the top of the bank, and the upper story of frame.

The shot tower is worthy of a description. It is built on the summit of a rocky hill on the bank of Pipe creek near its entrance into the Wisconsin. This hill has a perpendicular face next the creek, and a gentle descent southward, and westward, by which wagons may reach the summit. One hundred feet from the base of the rock, there is a ledge or landing place; on this ledge rises the shot tower, of frame, eighty feet to the roof; of course the depth from the top of the tower to the base of the rock is one hundred and eighty feet; a well or shaft has been sunk through the rock, which is of sand-stone, one hundred feet, and a lateral drift or entrance, ninety feet in length, seven feet high, and six feet wide, has been cut from the bank of the creek to the perpendicular shaft; a basin of seven feet deep is sunk below the surface of the entrance shaft; this basin is constantly supplied with water, into which the shot falls from the top of the tower, where the lead is melted and cast through the well or shaft.

A small rail-way is erected within the lateral drift, communicating with the well, and extending to the finishing house, which is built on the bank of the creek, immediately opposite the entrance to the shaft. On this rail-way the shot is carried in small boxes or cars from the basin or well, by a horse power, into the finishing house; this same power by various machinery is employed in drying the shot in a cylinder over an oven; from the oven the shot is carried into the polishing barrel, and thence the various sizes are passed over the several inclined floors for separation, and taken to the separating sieves; after which the several sizes are weighed, bagged, and put into kegs; a steamboat can lie at the door of the finishing house for the purpose of taking the commodity to market.

This establishment would do honour to any old settlement in the east; the public spirit of the proprietors deserves remuneration in the profits of their business. I am informed that five thousand weight of shot is the usual quantity made per diem, by *one set*, that is six hands—twice the quantity can be made by doubling the hands—of course there is no want of pigs of lead in this country. This company are the owners of a large body of mineral and timber land. One of the partners, Mr. Benjamin L. Webb, resides here, and superintends the concern. The hospitality of his house, and the information obtained in his society, are matters on which a traveller's recollection may dwell with pleasure.

From the shot tower hill, the view down the Wisconsin river, for thirty or forty miles, cannot be surpassed in beauty; the winding of the broad stream through and amongst the numerous wooded islands which cover its surface, until the bright sparklings of the water, seen at intervals in the almost interminable chain of islands, is totally lost in the distant horizon; the high and bold outline of the hills in the Indian country north of the river, and extending westward to the Mississippi, all present a delightful subject for a painter. Opposite to Helena and north of the Wisconsin is a most noble and beautiful tract of prairie, about five miles wide from the river to the hills, and extending up and down the river for more than ten miles; it is at present Indian country—the whites are prohibited from entering it to explore it—but its mineral and other advantages are supposed to be equal, if not superior to the south side of the river. This country will be ours shortly, as the Winnebagos cannot remain intermingled with white settlers, and no obstacle will stay the enterprise of our citizens. The Indians must sell their lands in this Territory.*

* This country has since been purchased by the United States, (1838.)

MINERAL POINT.

Description—Population—Distances—Executive and County Offices—Stores and Taverns—Buildings—Miners' Dwellings—Fine Spring—Additions to the Town—Mechanics—Miners—High Wages—Town Surveyed—Settlers' Claims—Country around—Mine Holes—Mineral Lands—Galena—Course of the Lead Trade—Miner and Smelter—Profit—Copper Mines—Great Product of the Diggings—Richness of the Ore—Value of the Mines.

Returning from Helena, and passing through Dodgeville and Dodge Grove, an excellent road over the prairie and a distance of twenty-four miles brings the traveller to Mineral Point. This place is by much the largest town in this district, and contains about fifteen hundred inhabitants. It is situated in the midst of the mineral region, thirty-eight miles from Galena, forty from Du Buque, and fifty from Madison. Here are the Executive Offices of the Territory and the Land Office for the Wisconsin Land District; it is also the county town of Iowa county, and of course the county offices are kept here. A charter for a bank has been granted to this place; but it is very doubtful if it will ever go into operation. In the town are seven dry goods stores, four public houses, four groceries and liquor stores, one brewery and about two hundred and fifty houses; a court-house and small jail are also here. Several new buildings are being erected, and the commissioners appointed by law are now laying out the streets, and establishing the correct lines of the several lots, according to the respective claims of the first settlers. By act of congress, a section of land was given to the town for public purposes, which will probably raise a fund of $10,000.

This town was commenced by the miners; they built their little log cabins along a straggling line, under the shelter of a hill, and near a small branch of the Peketonica. Hence the irregularity of buildings in the lower street; the buildings on the hill and in the new part of the town are of course better than the first dwellings of the hardy pioneers. One of the streets is laid out, up a small ravine, at the head of which a most delightful spring of water gushes forth, and passes through the ravine the whole length of the street. This spring has been covered over in a neat manner with mason work, to preserve its purity, and its usefulness to the inhabitants is justly valued. An addition to the present town has been laid off in lots on the hill south of this ravine; another addition has also been laid off in lots, west of the town; and the growing importance of Mineral Point, will doubtless soon bring this property into demand. Mechanics are much wanted here; there are now two tailor shops, one shoemaker, two smithies, two carpenter shops, and one cabinet-maker; certainly very few mechanics for so large a population. There are at least four hundred miners here, whose sole occupation is the exploration of mines, and the raising of mineral. A constant market is thus kept up for all productions of the farmer, and for all the necessaries of life. Prices are of course high, and labour also has its reward in high wages. I am informed that carpenters and stone-masons can earn three and four dollars per diem, and labouring hands can obtain two dollars from any farmer for a day's work in his harvest field. These prices may not continue long, but the demand for mechanics and labourers now, in all parts of the Territory, should be an inducement to the industrious population of the eastern states to cast their eyes on Wisconsin, as a land of promise that will not deceive.

The town is now accurately surveyed, and laid off in streets, and the lots of different size and shape have been surveyed according to the substantiated claims of the several original settlers and their representatives, consequently in the old part of the town the streets are neither uniform nor rectangular, but in the new parts the plan is well laid. With respect to the claims of the original settlers here, around the mines, the government has done well to acknowledge and protect them. Town lots not exceeding an acre each have been allowed to every original settler, at a nominal price of five dollars per lot. Those lands which were included in the grant for the town of Mineral Point, and which are not subject to entry, belong to the corporation. Rents are very high, and building expensive, owing to the present scarcity of lumber, and the want of mechanics. The price for town lots is various and depends on their location, ranging from one hundred to eight hundred dollars. The rich discoveries of lead and copper ore, in the immediate vicinity of Mineral Point, will always render it a place of extensive business.

The town takes its name from a hill, or extension of the upland prairie, lying east of the ravine, through which flows a branch of the Peketonica. On this hill, the *first* lead diggings were opened, and they still continue to be worked to great advantage. The hill divides two small branches of the Peketonica, and terminates abruptly south of the town, where the streams unite; hence the name of Mineral Point.

On the most eastern of these branches there is a neat furnace which does an excellent business; it is situated about half a mile from the town, over the hill. West of the town, about two miles, on the road to Diamond Grove, there are two excellent establishments of smelting furnaces, and other buildings, situate on one of the principal heads of the

Peketonica; about the same distance south of Mineral Point is the copper furnace of Mr. Ansley one of the proprietors of the copper mines; in O'Neill's grove, about three miles south-west of the town, is the lead furnace of J. F. O'Neill.

The most numerous lead diggings are on the high grounds, north and west of the town; these are worked even now to great advantage although the shafts are seldom more than forty or fifty feet deep; and as soon as *capital* is employed here in working these mines *properly*, and to the best *advantage*, I doubt not that the lead region of Wisconsin will be *known* as the richest and most productive of any in our country. It is evident that no sufficient exploration of the value and extent of any of the *leads* has yet been made—want of machinery, want of proper *openings* of mines, and above all, want of capital, have been great drawbacks on the prosperity of the Wisconsin lead mines; their richness has been universally acknowledged, and although individual enterprise has been hitherto exerted in a manner highly creditable to a new country, and a hardy population, yet most certainly the time is yet to arrive, when the mineral wealth of this interesting country shall be properly developed. That time cannot be far distant, and when it shall occur, we may look forward to a future prosperity of the miner and smelter not easily at this time to be calculated.

The country immediately around Mineral Point is broken into a number of small eminences and ravines; the hills are generally covered with hazel bushes, and although the soil is not of so good a quality as it is at a few miles distance, yet it is sufficiently rich to produce, with proper cultivation, in a degree equal to very many parts of the Territory, out of the rolling prairie districts. These hills are perfectly covered by the explorations of the miners, and indeed it is dangerous for the benighted traveller to wind his devious path amongst the excavations; he may without notice be instantaneously engulfed in a mine hole. These mineral lands have been excluded from private entry in the Land Office, and are worked at will by the miners, with an understanding by common consent among themselves, as to the extent around each *lead* or *prospect* which the discoverer may claim, as his exclusive right of digging and exploring. The Galena mineral here found, yields in smelting from seventy to eighty-five per cent. of pure lead, and consequently is equally profitable to the miner and the smelter. The course of trade is, that the miner raises the mineral from the bowels of the earth, and the smelter sends his teams to the mine, whence he draws the crude mineral to his furnace; by return teams he delivers to the order of the miner, *fifty per cent*. on what he receives of ore, in pig lead, and of course the smelter obtains from twenty to thirty-five per cent of lead as his profit by his smelting-furnace. From this profit is to be deducted his daily expense of fuel, payment of hands, keeping of stock, wear and tear of materials, implements and live stock, and also the interest of employed capital; a smelting-furnace that will yield from five thousand to seven thousand pounds of lead daily, and many are calculated to produce this result, must certainly be profitable.

About a mile and a half north-east of the town on the hills, which rise into the great prairie extending to the Blue mounds, are found the copper mines. Here has been raised immense bodies of copper ore which is said to yield from twenty to thirty per cent! an enormous product, when it is considered that the best mines of Europe are worked to great advantage on a yield of ten or twelve per cent. These copper mines I understand are owned by a company, whose operations have been cramped and suspended by reports relative to their richness and extent, which reports I am induced to believe have not been founded on accurate and judicious investigation. Much is due to these mines, and to the future prosperity of this whole section of country, in having them thoroughly and scientifically examined; expectation in regard to them has been greatly raised, and even a temporary depression in public feeling is of course much felt. I cannot hazard much in saying, that from the character of the mineral region, its geological peculiarities, and the hasty and imperfect observations which have been made relative to the copper mines at Mineral Point, this slight shade cast over their character will speedily be removed, and this interesting region yet have due justice done to its richness in copper as well as in lead; and that these mines will shortly be worked with great profit to the proprietors, and with general advantage to the United States. I have learnt from one of the proprietors that 58,000 pounds of this copper ore was shipped to England in the summer of 1836, which yielded *thirty-three* per cent.! There is now on the ground at the copper diggings more than five hundred tons of ore already raised, and if a market could be obtained for the sale of the ore, there are now at least one hundred experienced miners at this place who would cheerfully undertake to work these mines on shares. These men have had many years experience in Cornwall in England, in mining, and they pronounce these copper mines to have as favourable a prospect as any they have ever worked. The furnace of Mr. Ansley, in which twelve thousand pounds of copper has already been smelted *by a single process,* is not now in operation. No person sufficiently acquainted with copper smelting is yet in this part of the country, and of course the ore has not yet been worked to advantage. This copper brought in the Boston market twenty-two cents per pound; other copper sold at eighteen cents per pound. From my own judgment I should think that such an immense body of ore as has here been raised, from such small excavations, and in so limited a space of ground, gives the strongest assurances of the extent and value of these copper mines; no shaft has been yet sunk to a greater depth than fifty feet; certainly a fair trial has not yet been given to them, and, as I before observed, some injury has been done to their character by the hasty, crude and perhaps unscientific examination of them which has been made. The geological formation of the country should be well studied and understood, before any positive assertions are made respecting the copper mines of Wisconsin, at least to their detriment; positive assertions may well be made touching their richness, if quantity, and quality of ore, and ease of procuring it are any favourable circumstances.

8*

BELMONT.

Road from Mineral Point—Peketoniea—Great Prairie—Fine farms—Platte Mounds—Belmont—Town and Country—Description of the Mounds—Race Course—Beautiful and extensive view—Interesting picture—Platte Village and Mills.

The distance from Mineral Point to the Platte Mounds is about twelve miles; the road excellent, except two or three steep ascents of small hills, which may easily be amended, when the country becomes more settled, and road taxes raised, and greater attention paid to the leading thoroughfares of the country. About four or five miles from Mineral Point the road crosses two branches of the west Peketonica, flowing through wide natural meadows, about a mile and a half apart. These two branches unite a few miles to the south, at New Baltimore, the establishment of Richard M'Kim, Esq. The lands after leaving the Peketonica rise suddenly at the farm of Mr. Perry into the great prairie, which extends from Elk Grove northward to Parish's, at the heads of Blue river, and eastward from Parish's, past Dodgeville, to the Blue Mounds, the largest and richest agricultural tract, and at the same time one of the richest mineral regions that I have seen in the territory. Immediately on entering the prairie, several finely cultivated farms, particularly that of Mr. Westrope, are seen in various parts of the widely extended view; a ride of a few miles over a rich country brings the traveller to the foot of the easternmost of the Platte Mounds, and after passing about a mile and a half through a fine wood, around the northern base of the Mound, the neat village of Belmont, with its white painted houses and red roofs, forms a picturesque object, combined with the towering Mounds, and the green surrounding prairie. The town contains about half a dozen well built frame houses. This place has not increased rapidly in population. It was for one session of the legislature the seat of government, but the recent removal to Burlington, and the establishment of Madison as the future seat of government, has cast a temporary shade over Belmont. Towns may be projected, lots may be sold, houses may be built, but until the country becomes settled by an industrious population, and there shall be an adequate demand for mechanics, no town can prosper. *The country makes the town,* in all cases, except perhaps where the establishment of a manufactory may force a village into life, and in such instance, the town will *make the adjacent country,* if it be capable of cultivation. Belmont being situate on the great road leading from Galena through the territory to the lakes, and in the midst of so fine an agricultural country, must yet be a place of considerable importance. All that is wanting now, is the farming of the adjoining prairies, and the establishment of mechanics in the town.

The village is built near the foot of the eastern mound. The east and west mounds are about two miles distant. Their general elevation is about two hundred feet, and they are well covered with wood. Between the town and the western mound, the centre mound rises like a pyramid in the plain. This mound is covered with grass, bare of wood, and with the exception of a few jutting rocks near the summit, presents a regular surface from its base to its top. It rises from the prairie with a gentle ascent on all sides, about one-fourth of a mile from its base, until it abruptly assumes its conical form, and rises about fifty feet, when its apex, from a distance, appears completely a point, although a hundred persons may stand upon it. Around the second base is a circular race course of a little more than a mile, and well laid out; horse races are frequently run here: from the top of the mound a spectator might see a dog run all around the course. The view from this mound, as well as from the flat near the summit of the eastern mound, surpasses description! An ocean of prairie surrounds the gazer, whose vision is not limited to less than thirty or forty miles; this great sea of verdure is interspersed with delightfully varying undulations like the vast waves of the ocean, and every here and there sinking in the hollows, or cresting the swells, appear spots of wood, large groves, extensive ranges of timber, small groups of trees, as if planted by the hand of art, for ornamenting this naturally splendid scene! Over this extended view in all directions are scattered the incipient farms of the settlers, with their luxuriant crops of wheat and oats, whose yellow sheaves, already cut, form a beautiful contrast with the waving green of the Indian corn, and the smooth dark lines of the potato crop. Throughout the prairie the most gorgeous variety of flowers are seen rising above the thickly set grass, which in large and small patches has here and there been mowed for hay, all presenting a curious chequered appearance of the table beneath us. The mineral flower, the tall bright purple, and red feather, the sunflower, the yellow broom, the golden rod, the several small and beautiful flowers interspersed with the grass, render the scene indescribably beautiful. To the north the Wisconsin hills are seen bounding the view; to the east, prairie and wood are only limited by the horizon, and the Blue mounds on the north-east form a back ground and a land mark; to the south, the view over the rolling country extends into the state of Illinois; in the south-west is seen the Sinsinewa mound; the view to the west is only bounded by the Table mound, and the hills west of the Mississippi, and distant about thirty miles; whilst to the north-west the high hills through which the father of waters breaks his sweeping way, close the view. Below us, on the plain, is the little village of Belmont, with its bright painted dwellings; the brown lines in the broad green carpet indicate the roads and tracks over the prairie; the grazing cattle are scattered over the wide surface looking like sheep or dogs in size; whilst in the distance are seen travelling wagons of emigrants, and ox-teams hauling lead, merchandise, and lumber; the horseman and foot-traveller are passing and repassing; pleasure and travelling carriages are whirling rapidly over the sward, as if the country had been improved for a century past, instead of having been only five years reclaimed from the savages. This picture is not exaggerated; it fails of the original beauty, in the attempt to describe that scene which is worth a journey of a thousand miles to contemplate in the calm sunset of a summer day, as I have viewed it from the top of the Platte mounds.

About five miles from Belmont is the Platte village; I did not visit it, neither did I see the Platte mills, grist and saw-mills, which are in this neighbourhood, possessing considerable water power, and great bodies of excellent timber attached to them. Saw-mills being very few in the country, as yet, the trade in lumber at the Platte mills is abundant and lucrative, and will long remain so, as the timber is scarce on this beautiful prairie, and its soil is so excellent, that it must inevitably become a fine farming district.

THE PEKETONICA OR PEE-KE-TOL-I-KA.

New Baltimore—M'Kim's Furnace and establishment—Extent of the river—Wiota—Rich Meadows—Cedar Bluffs—Willow Springs—Public Roads—Farms—Bracken's—Sheldon's—Hospitalities—Intelligence of the Settlers—Books and Newspapers—Lead diggings—The Indian Reservations—Claims by Improvement—Otterbourne—Gratiot—The Peketonica Country—Hamilton—Indian Town—Rock River Improvements.

A SMALL branch of the Peketonica runs through a ravine or narrow meadow at Mineral Point, in a southern course, receiving in its way many fine springs, until it unites about five miles below the town with the main branch of the same river, about two miles above the furnace and establishment of Richard M'Kim, Esquire, to which he has given the name of New Baltimore. His smelting furnace, saw-mill, workmen's houses, and his mansion, are situate on the western bank of the Peketonica, which is here a considerable stream; a mile west of New Baltimore, flows another large branch, on which is built Kindle's grist-mill. The natural meadow at New Baltimore, and for several miles above, is unrivalled for fertility of soil, and beauty of scenery, not only in its own features, but in the general character of the hills and bluffs bounding the low land. The broad deep and clear Peketonica winds its way through the wide expanse of low and level prairie or meadow, covered with high grass, and composed of a soil which is complained of by cultivators as being *too rich* for any small grain, but which is unrivalled for the production of corn, potatoes, pumpkins, and all esculents. This meadow extends from the borders of Diamond Grove near Col. Bequette's, widening in its course southeastward, and bearing the several branches of the Peketonica on its bosom, as low down as the junction of the eastern branch, near the old Indian town of "Wiota," in the neighbourhood of the diggings of Col. William S. Hamilton, formerly of New York, but for some years a Wisconsin Pioneer. From Wiota the river, I am informed, is navigable, and indeed boats have been laden with lead and sent from New Baltimore, and from the Cedar Bluffs, about a mile below, by Mr. Charles Bracken. This is the most extensive range of fine meadow which I have visited, it is about thirty-five miles from Diamond Grove to the forks at Wiota, and a more delightfully beautiful and rich body of land, is not to be desired, than the country through which the Peketonica flows.

In the immediate neighbourhood of the Cedar Bluffs, about three miles from New Baltimore, is a small village called the Willow Springs. Here are three or four dwellings and the store of Mr. Dillon; an old smelting-furnace is also here, now disused, as it was built on the first plan called the "log and ash furnace." This crude manner of smelting lead by the earlier settlers, has given way to the improved cupola and oven furnace, and the blast furnace.

A great public road from Mineral Point to Gratiot's Grove passes by the Willow Springs, and this will always be a main road through this part of the territory, in its principal direction, with perhaps a few changes in parts, where experience will correct early adoptions of convenience.

Leaving the Willow Springs, and passing in a northern direction over a high prairie with oak openings, about three miles, the country becomes highly interesting. Here are to be found many farms in the best and most profitable state of cultivation. Farm-houses and barns and stables, with other out-houses, announce a good settlement, and that the farmer not only knows how to live, but does live well. The kindness and hospitality which I experienced during several days residence and excursions in this delightful section of country, will be held by me in heartfelt recollection. I need only mention the names of Messrs. Charles and John Bracken, and Major John P. Sheldon, in whose families I found myself at home, to justify my feelings. Not only in their domestic circles, intelligent conversation, good collections of books, and weekly receipts of news from the *far east*, did we find (Dr. Smith and myself) intellectual luxuries which were the more grateful because unexpected, but the readiness with which we were accompanied in our excursions through the country by these gentlemen, gave us not only the means and the comforts of travelling, but the information without which, as strangers, we should have been greatly deficient.

On the subject of attentions and hospitalities received by my son and myself during our stay in the country, and in very many excursions through it, I should be wanting not only in correct feelings of recognition of, but also in respect to, the many friends and acquaintances which we formed. Delicacy alone forbids me to speak publicly of the kindnesses we have at all times and in all places experienced. Prairie du Chien, Parish's, Messer Grove, Helena, Dodge's Grove, Mineral Point, New Baltimore, and other places live as bright spots on memory. The inhabitants and the inmates of those places named will duly appreciate the motives by which I am actuated when I forbear to say more.

It is worthy of remark that in all places where I have been in Wisconsin—in the comfortable dwelling-house in the town—in the snug and neat farm-house—in the log cabin, I have *always* found books and newspapers—of books, many standard and historical works, together with the new novels—of newspapers, those of New York, Baltimore, Washington, and Philadelphia were common, and generally the State papers of the *former home* of the Wisconsin emigrant. Amongst the literary papers I often found the excellent publications of our friends Godey and Alexander of Philadelphia; the "Saturday News" is much liked.

From the farm of Mr. Charles Bracken the road to Mineral Point passes over a part of the extensive prairie which reaches to the Blue Mounds, and on this road and near it, there are numerous valuable lead diggings, particularly those of Messrs. Bracken. South of Bracken's the main road to Dixon's ferry in Illinois, passes several excellent and well improved farms, particularly that of Major Sheldon. A mile or two south of Sheldon's we enter a fine body of woodland, called the Indian Reservations, surveyed for the half-breeds, but not, as is said, in conformity with the treaty, and consequently the surveys will be *lifted* and re-located.* These tracts are in number, in this neighbourhood, forty, of a mile square each, of course here is, in one body 25,600 acres of the finest timber land, and arable soil, in the Wisconsin Land District. This land will no doubt be in market shortly, and the farmer's

* This has since been done by order of the Indian Department. (1838.)

attention deserves to be turned to this part of the country. Claimants by improvement are already making their locations in these reservations, but the land having been reserved, and never offered for sale by the government, I think the existing pre-emption laws will not reach the cases of settlements on them made at this day, and such locations may be of no avail.

Passing through this well timbered country for about seven miles, the union of two branches of the Peketonica at a point of land, high and covered with wood, overlooking the beautiful natural meadow before described, is located the village of Otterbourne. This location is excellent; the advantages of wood, water, public roads, most excellent land and delightful scenery, give promise that Otterbourne will in time prosper—at any rate, it deserves to become a town; independent of the localities named, there is an excellent saw-mill and all convenient buildings, within a few hundred yards of the newly laid out town. This saw-mill has fine water power, and abundance of timber in the neighbourhood. Water powers for a grist-mill can be easily obtained here, and as far as my judgment goes, nature has done as much for this mill seat as for any I have seen in this district.

With such advantages, if a few good mechanics, blacksmiths, shoemakers, tailors, carpenters, stone-masons and labourers would seek their good, they may obtain town lots here at a very low rate, and the village of Otterbourne might thus spring immediately into life.

About seven miles below Otterbourne, on the Peketonica river, a beautiful and advantageous site has been selected for a town; it has been laid off in lots, and is called "Gratiot." At this point there is a saw-mill, and small grist-mill, designated as Sheldon's mills, although the grist-mill was built by the late Col. Henry Gratiot. This location possesses many advantages, there being a large body of good prairie land near it, yet unsold, and a considerable tract of timber land is also adjacent. This spot, by a great bend in the Peketonica river, is rendered the nearest point on that river to Galena, to which place there is already an excellent road the whole distance to within three or four miles of Galena, being on a prairie ridge. The proprietors of the mills contemplate erecting, during the next year, a stone grist-mill, in addition to the one now in operation; the water-power for the works is furnished by Wolf creek, which empties into the Peketonica at this place.

The Peketonica country is one of the best watered sections I have seen; the various branches traverse delightful prairies, and rich bottom lands, over a wide extent of country. Fine water powers are numerous on these branches; and on the union of the east and the west branches, a few miles below

"Hamilton" at Wiota, the old Indian town of Winno-shek, a chief of the Winnebagoes, a noble river is formed. This stream, after receiving Sugar river, empties into Rock river, a few miles below the territorial line, in Winnebago county, Illinois. The improvement of the rapids of Rock river, for which an appropriation of $100,000 has been lately made by the Illinois legislature, will go far to render this river perfectly safe for steamboat navigation. The General Government owes this section of country efficient aid, as a matter of *general importance*, more than of *local* appropriation.

ELK GROVE.

Highly cultivated Farms—Clinton—Advantages of Elk Grove
—Prairies.

Pursuing the great road from Belmont to Galena, over the fertile and extensive prairie so often mentioned, at about seven miles distance from the Platte mounds southward, the traveller enters Elk Grove. Here are several fine farms in the highest state of cultivation, with excellent and commodious improvements and buildings. At the northern entrance into the grove, are the establishments of J. Hollman, Esq., Chief Justice Dunn, Mr. W. I. Madden, a son-in-law of Governor Dodge, who has a fine smelting-furnace, and also the farms of many other settlers, amongst which is the highly improved farm of Major Legate of Galena, formerly superintendent of the lead mines. This farm is under excellent post and rail fence, with good farm houses and barns, thriving young orchards, and about three hundred acres of land in fine order and cultivation; clover is here used with great advantage to the fields and the stock; there are about thirty good settlements made in and around the grove, and still a large body of the best land to be worked remains in its natural state. This grove has been one of the best timbered in this district, and although partially *thinned* of wood, at this time, by reason of the timber having been for some years used for smelting purposes, there is yet a very large extent of heavy timber remaining. I here saw the largest white-oak and black walnut that I met with in the territory. Towards the southern part of the grove is a good house of public entertainment, and here also is a village laid out called "Clinton." The head waters of Fevre river, which is navigable for steamboats as far as Galena, rise in this grove. For beauty of prospects, fertility of soil, fine springs, and abundance of excellent timber, Elk Grove has not its superior situation in this part of the country; add to its natural advantages the constant purity of atmosphere, and consequent health to the inhabitants, and this section of country holds out every inducement to the farmer, or emigrant of fortune, who desires a delightful residence in an excellent and intelligent neighbourhood, to settle here. If I purchase in this country for my future permanent residence, it shall be in this quarter; many very desirable locations can still be obtained on the borders of the grove, in the prairie, with small portions of timber attached, but the whole of the grove I believe has been already *entered* in the land office.

GALENA.

Fevre River—Importance of Galena—Great trade—Ferry—Description of the Town—Steamboats—Newspapers of Wisconsin Territory.

From this place to Galena, the road passes over a continuous high and rolling prairie for about twelve or fourteen miles, when it crosses the Illinois state line, and about six miles farther abruptly descends the high grounds, and the flourishing town of Galena appears, hanging, as it were, on the side of a precipitous hill, and stretched along a narrow, deep, and tortuous stream called Fevre (or Bean) river. The depth of water in this river is principally caused by the back-water of the Mississippi. Steamboats ascend this river from the Mississippi, distant about six miles to its mouth, although in a western line from Galena, over land, the river is reached in about two and a half miles.

The town of Galena has been, and still is, the great mart for the shipment of the lead and agricultural productions of Wisconsin, that is on the eastern side of the river; Dubuque on the western side has always enjoyed a considerable share of the steamboat trade. Galena, from its situation on Fevre river, at the head of the navigation, besides being the southern outlet of the fertile country in Wisconsin, lying in parts of Grant, Iowa, and Green counties, will continue to increase with the settlement of the upper country, and its consequent increased trade. Some idea may be formed of the extent of business in Galena at this time, when I observe, that I counted *sixty-two stores* on the street stretching along the bank of Fevre river. Many of these stores are of the first order, and possessing large capital; the stir and bustle of business, the influx of market and farm wagons, the ponderous ox teams drawing the lead to its place of shipment, the rattling of carts, drays, hackney coaches and carriages along this street, announce the present and growing importance of Galena.

There is a ferry established here over Fevre river, crossed by means of a rope, and it may truly be said, that the boat is never idle—every five or ten minutes in the day, foot passengers, horsemen, carts, wagons and carriages, are passing and re-passing. It is certainly very desirable that a bridge should be built here, and there is an excellent site for one, above the steamboat landing, and near the beautiful dwelling of Mr. J. P. B. Gratiot.

The upper street of the town is hung on the face of a high and steep hill—the two principal public houses are in this street; it is difficult for loaded wagons to ascend this hill from the lower to the upper street; but at either end of the upper street the entrances have been cut down, and through the hill, so as to render the approach on a level with the roads descending from the upper country into the town; much improvement in filling up, levelling, curbing and paving the streets with stone, and with brick side-ways, is daily going forward; an extensive wharf along the Fevre river, affording a range of quays with inlets to the cross streets, is now commenced, and when finished will give an impetus in regard to business facilities to Galena, which its important and eligible location, its present and increasing trade, and the enterprise and public spirit of its citizens well deserve.

The new buildings in the town, particularly some stone warehouses in the lower, and many brick private dwellings in the upper street, are in the best taste, regarding size, conveniences and finishing; the want of gardening ground may be considered as an objection, but I observed several hanging gardens, above the dwellings, on the upper street, and they may readily be made in many parts, on the face of the hill; on the whole, Galena, with all its rough looking surrounding hills is an interesting point in the far west, and its growing importance and future prosperity may safely be predicted.

Steamboats arrive and depart several times during the week, from and to the lower and the upper country of the Mississippi. The elegant and commodious boat "Missouri Fulton" is now here, Dr. Smith and myself will depart in her to-morrow or next day; and if we have a prosperous voyage down to St. Louis, and up the Ohio to Pittsburg, we confidently hope to meet you within twelve days or two weeks at the farthest, in your goodly city of Philadelphia.

I shall embody a few remarks relative to the statistics of the Territory, which I have gleaned from several sources, particularly the newspapers of Wisconsin. For the honour of the citizens of this Territory, they have already afforded support to the following weekly newspapers: the Iowa News, published at Du Buque; the Miners' Free Press, published at Mineral Point; the Wisconsin Territorial Gazette, published at Burlington; the Milwaukee Advertiser, published at Milwaukee; the Wisconsin Democrat, published at Green Bay, and the Western Adventurer, published at Montrose, or Old Fort Des Moines. All these papers are well conducted, and in point of size and contents, they may stand in competition with any of the papers of the old states.

ADDENDA.

STATISTICS AND OBSERVATIONS.

Population of the Territory—Western Wisconsin—Spirit of Speculation—Counties in the Territory—Wisconsin Land District—Legislature—Executive—Secretary—Judiciary—Appointments of Officers of Government, Salaries—Delegate to Congress—Appropriation for Public Buildings—Education Funds—Towns on the right bank of the Mississippi—Distance from St. Louis, and Population—Distance from Pittsburg to the Falls of St. Anthony—Towns on the left bank of the Mississippi—Distance from St. Louis and Population—Post Offices in the Territory.

THE following statement of the population of the Wisconsin Territory is taken from the reports made to the Governmental Department, as the correct census in 1836.

Brown county,	2706
Milwaukee county,	2893
Iowa county,	5234
Crawford county,	850
Du Buque county,	4274
Des Moines county,	6257
	22,214

At this time, it is believed that the population on the west side of the river is equal to, if not exceeding, the whole number in 1836; and on the east side, although the tide of emigration has not been so strong as in the Black Hawk purchase, we may perhaps safely say that Eastern Wisconsin has a population at this time of about 20,000; and Iowa, or the district west of the river, of about 25,000. The increase is daily, and already efforts are being made to divide the Territory; surveyors are now in the Black Hawk purchase, laying off the public lands; these lands will soon be in market; the country will quickly fill up, and if laid off as a separate Territory, Western Wisconsin may become a new state in the Union, before the Eastern Territory is ready to apply. The emigration to the western side of the river was greatly increased in consequence of the spirit of speculation having been so widely and destructively diffused over the eastern part of the Territory. Immense bodies of fine lands were seized on by individuals, and companies of purchasers, who having had *banking facilities* at command, could embrace some hundred thousand acres in their entries, and deluge the Land Office with showers of *bank promises to pay*. The specie circular of the Secretary of the Treasury fortunately and opportunely, for the future prosperity of the Territory, checked the growing evil—but enough mischief has been done to retard for many years the increase of the eastern section equally with the west. The industrious emigrant finds many of the best lands in the hands of the speculator, and he is compelled to move onward to the west, until he can settle on lands to which he may have his pre-emption right, or at least be able to purchase at government price, without being obliged to purchase at an enhanced price from the capitalist.

By an act of the legislature of 1836, the following counties were laid off; some of these counties are divisions of the old ones, and others are bounded, as the increased population demanded.

Counties laid off in 1836.

Des Moines,	Lee,	Van Buren,
Henry,	Louisa,	Musquetine,
Cook,	Walworth,	Racine,
Jefferson,	Dane,	Portage,
Dodge,	Washington,	Cheboiegan,
Fond du Lac,	Calumet,	Manitoowoc,
Marquette,	Rock,	Iowa,
Grant,	Green,	Milwaukee,
Brown,	Crawford,	Du Buque.

Since the above was written, during the present Session of the Legislature, the county of Dubuque has been laid off in thirteen other counties, (1838) viz:

Clayton,	Jackson,	Benton,
Linn,	Jones,	Clinton,
Johnson,	Scott,	Delaware,

Buchanan, Cedar, Fayette, Keokuk.

The Wisconsin Land District contains 2,245,942 acres. Of this quantity, since the opening of the Land Office in October 1834, there have been sold 551,191 acres, and there remains to be sold 1,694,751 acres.

The Legislature of Wisconsin is composed of twenty-six members of the House of Delegates, and thirteen members of council; they are restricted by the organic law of Congress, in the duration of their session; they cannot sit more than seventy-five days in one session. The representatives are elected for two years and the council for four years. The governor is appointed for three years, unless sooner removed by the President. The secretary of the Territory is appointed for four years. The right of suffrage is extended to all white male citizens over twenty-one years of age. The members of both Houses are to be elected according to the ratio of population.

The judicial power is vested in a Supreme Court, District and Probate Courts, and in Justices of the Peace. The Supreme Court consists of a chief justice and two associate judges, to hold their offices during good behaviour. It is to meet annually at the seat of government. Each of the Supreme Judges is also to hold a District Court.

Judicial Officers, Justices of the Peace, Sheriffs

and Militia Officers are appointed by the Governor, by and with the advice and consent of the Council. Township and County Officers are elected by the people. Clerks of Courts are appointed by the Judges.

Salaries. Governor, $2,000, and as Superintendent of Indian affairs, $1,500; Secretary, $1,200; Judges each $1,800; Members of Legislature $3 per day and $3 for every twenty miles travelling.

A Delegate to Congress is elected by the people. The present Delegate is Col. George Wallace Jones, whose residence is at Sinsinewa mounds, a few miles from the Territorial line, near Galena.

Congress appropriated $20,000 for the erection of public buildings, and $5,000 for the purchase of a library, at the Seat of Government.

An act of the Legislature has established a University at Belmont,* and as the sixteenth section of every township of six miles square, has been reserved for public schools, there will be a permanent fund of six hundred and forty acres in each township for the purposes of education. These sections are generally of good land, and often of very valuable timber, their location, from the number, is consequently about the centre of each township.

The following is a list of towns on the Missis-

* By an act of the Legislature of December 1837, Wisconsin University is established at Green Bay; also a College at Mount Pleasant, in Henry county.

STATISTICS AND OBSERVATIONS.

sippi, on the right bank, above St. Louis, with their distance, and population in 1837.

Names.	Distance.	Population.
Portage des Sioux, Missouri,	33 miles,	500
Gideon,	60	20
Witherington,	70	15
Clarksville,	95	140
Louisiana,	105	300
Saverton,	130	100
Hannibal,	141	600
Scipio,	144	4
Marion City,	151	250
La Grange,	171	220
Tully,	179	100
Churchville,	195	8
Keokuk, Wisconsin Territory,	206	50
Montrose,	221	59
Fort Madison,	232	800
Burlington,	252	1200
Musquetine,	300	
Bloomington,	315	150
Geneva,	320	45
Salem,	324	50
Iowa,	329	3
Buffalo,	338	40
Montevideo,	343	5
Rockingham,	346	250
Davenport,	349	115
Le Claire,	366	

STATISTICS AND OBSERVATIONS.

Parkhurst,	367	20
Wisconsin City,	373	4
Camanche City,	387	240
New York,	395	6
Buellsburg,	398	15
Carlport,	416	8
Bellevue,	441	80
Du Buque,	470	1600
Prairie la Porte,	517	11
Fort Snelling, about		800 U. S. Post.

The distance from Pittsburg to the mouth of the Ohio river, is about 987 miles, thence up the Mississippi to St. Louis is about 250 miles, total distance from Pittsburg to St. Louis, 1237 miles, and thence to the Falls of St. Anthony about 807 miles, making the total distance from Pittsburg to the Falls 2044 miles.

The following is a list of the towns on the Mississippi, on the left bank, above St. Louis, with their distance and population in 1837.

Names.	Distance.	Population.
Chippewa, Illinois,	18 miles,	20
Alton, upper and lower,	24	4500
Grafton,	40	500
Milan,	46	30
Hamburg,	80	100
Quincy,	161	1600
Warsaw,	201	600
Montebello,	206	16

STATISTICS AND OBSERVATIONS.   117

Webster,	-	-	-	-	207	14
Commerce,	-	-	-	-	222	12
Appanoose,	-	-	-	-	232	180
Spilmernstown,	-	-	-		236	13
Oquako,	-	-	-	-	267	50
Kietsburg,	-	-	-		277	6
New Boston,		-	-	-	285	130
Bellefonte,	-	-	-		321	500
Rockport,	-	-	-	-	338	4
Stephenson,	-	-	-		342	900
Macneil,	-	-	-	-	354	18
Port Byron,	-	-	-		366	100
Canaan,	-	-	-	-	367	6
Albany,	-	-	-	-	390	90
Fulton City,	-	-	-	-	398	7
Savannah,	-	-	-	-	418	130
Huntsville,	-	-	-	-	433	11
Galena,	-	-	-	-	451	3000
Mississippi City, Wisconsin,				-	465	
Cassville,	-	-	-	-	505	500
Prairie du Chien,	-	-	-		539	600

A list of all the Post Offices established in the Territory of Wisconsin.

Names of Post Offices east of the Mississippi.

Mineral Point,   Iowa County.
Bellemont,   "

118   STATISTICS AND OBSERVATIONS.

Elk Grove,	Iowa County.
Dodgeville,	"
Helena,	"
Moundville,	"
Arena,	"
Mill-Seat Bend,	"
Diamond Grove,	"
Blue River,	"
Wingville, same Office,	"
Parish's, do.	"
English Prairie, (Savannah,)	"
White Oak Springs,	"
Willow Springs,	"
Wisconsin,	"
Gratiot's Grove,	"
Wiota,	"
Otterburn,	"
Cassville,	Grant Co.
Platteville,	"
Lancaster, (late La Fayette,)	"
Sinsinewa Mound,	"
Van Buren,	"
Blast Furnace,	"
Gibraltar,	"
Centreville,	"
Prairie du Chien,	Crawford Co.
Fort Snelling,	"
Madison, Dane Co.	(attached to Iowa Co.)
City of Four Lakes, (dis.)	"

New Mexico,	Green Co.
Jonesville,	Rock Co.
Outlet of Kuskenong,	"
Delevan,	Walworth Co.
Franklin,	"
Racine,	Racine Co.
Oak Creek,	"
Pike,	"
Mount Pleasant,	"
Aurora,	"
Pleasant Prairie,	"
Rochester,	"
Foxville,	"
Springfield,	not known.
Troy,	"
Milwaukee,	Milwaukee Co.
Prairie Village,	"
Washington,	Washington Co.
Cheboiegan,	Cheboiegan Co.
Manitoowoc,	Manitoowoc Co.
Fond du Lac,	Fond du Lac Co.
City of Winnebago,	Calumet Co.
Pipe Village,	"
Jefferson, (Atzland,)	Jefferson Co.
Fort Winnebago,	Portage Co.
Green Bay,	Brown Co.
Menomonie,	"
Grand Kakalin,	"
Butte des Morts,	"
Dupere,	"

STATISTICS AND OBSERVATIONS.

Post Offices west of the Mississippi.

Dubuque Mines,	Du Buque Co.
Bellevue,	"
Peru,	"
Durango,	"
Weyman's,	"
Salisbury,	"
Higginsport,	"
Parkhurst,	"
Pleasant Valley,	"
Wabesepinicon,	"
Davenport,	"
Rockingham,	Muscatine Co.
Clark's Ferry,	"
Iowa, (Mouth of Pine,)	"
Burlington,	Des Moines Co.
Gibson's Ferry,	"
Fort des Moines, (Montrose,)	"
Richland,	"
Fort Madison,	Lee Co.
Keokuk,	"

THERMOMETER.

D. M.	D. W.	6 A. M.	2½ P. M.	6 P. M.	WINDS.	WEATHER.
AUGUST 26	Sat.	73°	83°	78°	N. W.	Variable
27	Sun.	69°	80°	81°		,,
28	Mon.	72°	78°	79°	S. W.	Cloudy
29	Tues.	76°	94°	83°	S.	Clear
30	Wed.	74°	81°	72°		Cloudy
31	Thur.	58°	78°	68°	S. E.	Clear
SEPTEMBER 1	Frid.	55°	70°	72°		,,

DU BUQUE PRICES CURRENT.

Bacon—hog round,	10 a 12 cts per lb.
Hams,	12 a 13 "
Butter—Keg,	20 a 25 "
Fresh,	31 "
Candles—Dipped,	16 a 18 "
Sperm.	62 "
Coffee—Rio,	20 "
St. Domingo,	17 a 18 "
Flour—Superfine,	$12 a 15 per bbl.
Fine,	8 a 9 "
Corn-Meal,	1 25 a 1 50 per bush.
Fruit—Apples, dried,	2 00 "
Peaches,	3 50 "
Pared,	5 00 "
Grain—Corn,	1 25 "
Oats,	1 25 "
Hides—Green,	2 a 3 per lb.
Dry,	6 "
Nails and Spikes,	8d, 6d, 5d, 4d, 3d, 12½ cents.
	10d, 12d, 15d, 20d, 10 "
Lard—In Kegs,	15 cents per lb.
Lead—Pig,	4 "
Pork—Mess,	22 00 per bbl.
Prime,	18 00 "
Spices—Pepper,	31 "
Alspice,	31 "
Cloves,	75 "

Ginger,	25 cents per lb.
Nutmegs,	2 50 "
Sugars—New Orleans,	10 a 12 "
Havana,	12 "
Lump,	20 "
Loaf,	25 "
Teas—Young Hyson,	1 25 "
Imperial,	1 50 "
Gunpowder,	1 50 "
Black,	62 "
Tobacco—Cavendish,	75 "
Plug,	50 "

Lumber and building materials are in great demand. Labourers much wanted. Wages from 20 to 25 dollars per month and boarded. Hauling high. Four and five dollars per acre for breaking prairie sward.

Mineral has been sold lately at 15 dollars per thousand pounds.

CASSVILLE.

Cassville, on the left bank of the Mississippi, is certainly one of the most flourishing towns in the upper country. It contains at this time about forty excellent buildings, amongst which, the enterprising proprietors of the town, have lately erected an extensive Hotel which is said to have cost $70,000.

The town is situate on a beautiful level plain, about fifteen feet above low water mark; this bottom land is about four hundred and fifty yards wide, from the river to a bluff about two hundred feet high. The highland runs parallel with the Mississippi, for a considerable distance, and it is easily ascended by means of several ravines, in which good roads are made. From the top of the bluff a wide extent of fertile country spreads to the eastward, northward, and southward, and the view over the Mississippi, is really beautiful. The river here does not exceed half a mile in width, and there are fine steamboat landings along the front of the town. This narrowing of the river is remarkable at a place called "Mendota or Mississippi Landing," lying between Cassville and Prairie du Chien, on the right bank; here the river is very deep, clear of islands, and is not more than a quarter of a mile wide.

Cassville must flourish as a town and place of business; its situation on the river, and at the outlet of a fine agricultural and mineral region, give it advantages which may render it a formidable rival with Galena. The enterprise of its citizens is a praiseworthy example to the other parts of the Territory.

IOWA TERRITORY.

The following remarks have been furnished me by P. H. Engle, Esq., of Dubuque, and give a condensed view of the growing prosperity of the western side of the river Mississippi.

That portion of Wisconsin Territory which lies west of the Mississippi river extends on the west to Missouri and White Earth rivers, on the north to the Canada line, and on the south to the northern boundary of the State of Missouri. This is an immense tract of country, sufficient in extent to form four or five states. To a very small portion of these however, has the Indian title, as yet, been extinguished. After the successful termination of the Sac and Fox war by General Dodge in 1832, a treaty was made with those confederated tribes at Rock Island by General Scott, by which they ceded to the United States a strip of land on the west bank of the Mississippi river, about 50 miles in width, and extending from the Des Moines river to a point on the Mississippi about 40 miles north of the mouth of Turkey river. This, in the country, and in the neighbouring states of Illinois, Indiana and

Missouri is very usually called "the Black Hawk Purchase." By a treaty just ratified by the Senate of the United States, an important and valuable addition has been made to the lands which are now open to the settlement of the whites in this "District." It comprises about   acres, lies immediately west of the purchase first made; the main body of it west, or about west from Rock Island.

The lands thus newly acquired are represented by those who are enabled to make their statements from personal observation, to be extremely fertile and desirable; small prairies with fine groves of timber, well watered and in every respect well adapted to agricultural purposes. The first settlements formed by the whites in the "Iowa District," were in the summer of 1833; the population, as ascertained by the census taken in August, 1836, was about 11,000; the present population is variously estimated from 25 to 40,000; perhaps it would be safe to set it down at 30,000. A single fact will show what an important part of the immense tide of emigration which is now peopling the Mississippi Valley with such unexampled rapidity, has been flowing into this delightful region. A register was kept of the number of emigrant families transported into the Iowa District, at a single ferry on the Mississippi river, and it was found that from the 1st of April to the 1st of October, 1837, more than 1,800 *families* had been carried over at that one point. This alone, would probably bring a direct accession to the population of this section of the country in one summer of 9000 souls. To those who have seen and know the country, this rapid increase is not surprising. The writer knows of no section of country which offers greater inducement to emigration than this. In the first place, it is a good and healthy climate, free in a great measure from the numberless forms of billious and intermittent fevers which infest new countries in more southern latitudes. This may be said generally of the whole country; the exceptions are to be found only in a few of the towns and low places on the Mississippi and other large streams in the southern part of the "District." The soil is extremely fertile, equalling in this respect the best prairies in Illinois or elsewhere, and, particularly in the southern part, the prairies are small, with convenient groves of timber, and the country throughout is supplied with abundant streams of pure and wholesome spring water. The mineral wealth of this region forms also another powerful inducement to those "who are seeking their fortune" in the far west, to make this country their home. The lead mines in the neighbourhood of Dubuque have proved immense sources of wealth and prosperity to those who have embarked in that business, and have given an impetus to trade and improvement in that quarter which has not been surpassed in any other section of the western country.

The principal streams which water this country are the Des Moines, the Iowa, the Skunk, the Wabes-i-pin-i-con, the Macoquetais, and the Turkey. The Iowa is navigable for small class steamboats 150 miles; the navigation of the Des Moines is obstructed by rapids not far from its mouth, which, it is believed, can be remedied without much expense and labour. The Skunk, and one or two others have been *meandered* or surveyed, and they all afford copious supplies of timber for lumber, fencing and fuel, and they, with their numerous tributaries, give water power sufficient for mills of every description.

There are upwards of twenty towns and villages on the west bank of the Mississippi between the mouths of Des Moines and Turkey river. Of these the most important in point of population and present improvement are Dubuque, Burlington, Fort Madison, Bloomington, Bellevue, Rockingham and Davenport. Dubuque is in latitude 42° 30 north, nearly opposite the northern boundary of the state of Illinois, and is located on a small prairie, chiefly of sand, which has been formed between the bluff and the Mississippi, about thirty feet above the common level of the river, secure from inundation at the highest stages of water which have ever yet been known. Its present population is 1600.

Dubuque is in the centre of a rich and extensive mineral region, and from its position and natural advantages must some day be a place of very considerable importance. One unaccustomed to the rapidity with which towns spring up in the west, will be surprised to learn that the first improvement made in this place by the whites, was only about four years ago, and that it was only evacuated by the Indians in the summer of 1833. A newspaper was established at Dubuque in the spring of 1836, which is still continued, and is now called the "Iowa News." The "Miners Bank of Dubuque," chartered by the Legislative Assembly of the Territory and sanctioned by Congress, was put into operation in November, 1837. The Catholics have erected and completed (or very nearly so) a large and very handsome stone chapel, and a commodious and respectable-looking Presbyterian meeting-house built of hewed stone is now in progress, and wants only the completion of the inside work to be ready for its congregation. This will be done, it is said, early in the spring. The Methodists have also a meeting-house in the town.

Burlington, the present temporary seat of government of the Territory, is situated on the west bank of the Mississippi river, in latitude about 40° 45' north, in Des Moines county. Its situation is good, extremely so, and its landing for steamboats is one of the best on the river. Its population is about 12 or 15 hundred. The last session of the Legislative Assembly terminating on the 20th of January 1838, was held at this place. A spacious Hotel, sufficient for the accommodation of 60 or 80 persons, was erected last summer by an enterprising citizen of the place, and is now well conducted by Mr. and Mrs. Lockwood, formerly of Pittsfield, Massachusetts. The large edifice erected by Major Jeremiah Smith, for the accommodation of the Legislative Assembly, was unfortunately destroyed by fire during the session, together with five adjacent store-houses. There is energy and enterprise in the place sufficient in a very short time to repair this loss.

The country immediately back of Burlington is among the best for agricultural purposes in the "Mississippi Valley," and for several miles round is so thickly settled and highly improved, as to wear already somewhat of the aspect of an old country. There can be little doubt but that Burlington will be one of the largest places on the Mississippi river above St. Louis.

The writer does not wish to extend these remarks beyond a very limited compass, and therefore will say nothing of Fort Madison, Bloomington, Rockingham and Davenport, except that they are all beautiful and thriving villages and desirable places of residence to the enterprising emigrant.

A bill is now reported in Congress for the establishment of a new Territory out of that portion of Wisconsin lying west of the Mississippi river, to be called the Territory of Iowa. This name is derived from one of the principal rivers which empties into the Mississippi only a short distance above Burlington. This bill will become a law at the present session, without much doubt. The geographical position, and extent of the present Territory of Wisconsin, the pressing wants of a majority of the people of the whole Territory residing on the west side, the interests and wishes of the whole people on both sides, render it a measure of such obvious necessity and justice, that it can scarcely fail to receive the sanction of Congress, if they have time to act upon it. None of the land in the "Iowa District" has yet been offered for sale by the government; in fact the surveys are not yet entirely completed, of course the people are all "squatters;" but he who supposes that these settlers on the public lands, whose enterprise has led them to seek a home in the "Far West," and who are now building upon, fencing, and cultivating the lands of the government, are lawless depredators, devoid of the sense of moral honesty; or that they are not in every sense as estimable citizens, with as much intelligence, regard for law and social order, for public justice and private right, and as much patriotism as the farmers and yeomen of the states of New York and Pennsylvania, is very much mistaken, and has been led astray by vague and unfounded notions, or by positively false information.

In addition to the above remarks, the following account is extracted from the Territorial Gazette, published at Burlington.

Burlington is situate upon the west shore of the Mississippi river, in the county of Des Moines, of which it is the seat of justice, and Territory of Wisconsin, of which it is the temporary seat of government. It is about midway between the city of St. Louis and Galena, and between the two Rapids. Its location is beautiful and commanding. The river shore is some 15 or 18 feet above high water mark, and the land for half a mile back gently rises to perhaps fifty feet, from whence the prospect is extensive and very beautifnl—it is skirted with a fine grove of thriving timber, of almost every species, for a mile and a half, where the prairie commences. This vicinity has greatly the advantage of most, if not all the upper Mississippi country, in having an abundance of timber for every purpose—fine running water for manufacturing, and just a proper and convenient portion of prairie for grazing and farming purposes. The pump and well water in town for culinary and other purposes is excellent—it is clear, pure and cold. Burlington is now but little more than three years old and contains a population of 1200 souls. The increase during the last twelve months has been nearly, if not quite, one hundred per cent., and in the country adjacent, it has been even greater. Since the first day of April last, a period of but little more than three months, eighty odd buildings, most of them neat, and of good materials, and all comfortable, have been commenced—thirty-three dwellings of the above number, are already finished and occupied—forty more rapidly progressing—and ten warehouses, and stores, a church, a school, and a building (a capitol) for the accommodation of the Legislature at its next session, are also rapidly under way. The population of the town consists of emigrants from the eastern, middle and western states, and of almost every profession and calling—lawyers, doctors, merchants, mechanics, and farmers. There are eleven dry goods stores, well supplied with every article in that line of business, and disposed of upon reasonable and fair terms; twelve commission and groceries; two hotels for the accommodation of travellers and others, besides several boarding houses; two apothecary shops; two cabinet shops; one carriage and plough manufactory; one saddlery; one bakery; one boot and shoe-maker; one hatter; one silversmith and watch maker; one gunsmith; two tailors; one victualler and a painter; and there may, perhaps, be other arts and artizans who do not now occur to us. We have, also, here the Territorial Library, which is creditable to the Territory, and an ornament to the town. For the convenience of the public we have a livery stable, and a printing office, at which is printed *a most excellent newspaper, which we, with great disinterestedness,* commend to the patronage of the public. We have also, (and we had almost forgotten it, though it is a most important matter,) a steam ferry boat, which plies across the river.

MID-AMERICAN FRONTIER

An Arno Press Collection

Andreas, A[lfred] T[heodore]. **History of Chicago.** 3 volumes. 1884-1886

Andrews, C[hristopher] C[olumbus]. **Minnesota and Dacotah.** 1857

Atwater, Caleb. **Remarks Made on a Tour to Prairie du Chien: Thence to Washington City, in 1829.** 1831

Beck, Lewis C[aleb]. **A Gazetteer of the States of Illinois and Missouri.** 1823

Beckwith, Hiram W[illiams]. **The Illinois and Indiana Indians.** 1884

Blois, John T. **Gazetteer of the State of Michigan, in Three Parts.** 1838

Brown, Jesse and A. M. Willard. **The Black Hills Trails.** 1924

Brunson, Alfred. **A Western Pioneer: Or, Incidents of the Life and Times of Rev. Alfred Brunson.** 2 volumes in one. 1872

Burnet, Jacob. **Notes on the Early Settlement of the North-Western Territory.** 1847

Cass, Lewis. **Considerations on the Present State of the Indians, and their Removal to the West of the Mississippi.** 1828

Coggeshall, William T[urner]. **The Poets and Poetry of the West.** 1860

Darby, John F[letcher]. **Personal Recollections of Many Prominent People Whom I Have Known.** 1880

Eastman, Mary. **Dahcotah: Or, Life and Legends of the Sioux Around Fort Snelling.** 1849

Ebbutt, Percy G. **Emigrant Life in Kansas.** 1886

Edwards, Ninian W[irt]. **History of Illinois, From 1778 to 1833: And Life and Times of Ninian Edwards.** 1870

Ellsworth, Henry William. **Valley of the Upper Wabash, Indiana.** 1838

Esarey, Logan, ed. **Messages and Letters of William Henry Harrison.** 2 volumes. 1922

Flower, George. **The Errors of Emigrants.** [1841]

Hall, Baynard Rush (Robert Carlton, pseud.). **The New Purchase: Or Seven and a Half Years in the Far West.** 2 volumes in one. 1843

Haynes, Fred[erick] Emory. **James Baird Weaver.** 1919

Heilbron, Bertha L., ed. **With Pen and Pencil on the Frontier in 1851: The Diary and Sketches of Frank Blackwell Mayer.** 1932

Hinsdale, B[urke] A[aron]. **The Old Northwest: The Beginnings of Our Colonial System.** [1899]

Johnson, Harrison. **Johnson's History of Nebraska.** 1880

Lapham, I[ncrease] A[llen]. **Wisconsin:** Its Geography and Topography, History, Geology, and Mineralogy. 1846

Mansfield, Edward D. **Memoirs of the Life and Services of Daniel Drake.** 1855

Marshall, Thomas Maitland, ed. **The Life and Papers of Frederick Bates.** 2 volumes in one. 1926

McConnel, J[ohn] L[udlum.] **Western Characters:** Or, Types of Border Life in the Western States. 1853

Miller, Benjamin S. **Ranch Life in Southern Kansas and the Indian Territory.** 1896

Neill, Edward Duffield. **The History of Minnesota.** 1858

Parker, Nathan H[owe]. **The Minnesota Handbook, For 1856-7.** 1857

Peck, J[ohn] M[ason]. **A Guide for Emigrants.** 1831

Pelzer, Louis. **Marches of the Dragoons in the Mississippi Valley.** 1917

Perkins, William Rufus and Barthinius L. Wick. **History of the Amana Society.** 1891

Rister, Carl Coke. **Land Hunger:** David L. Payne and the Oklahoma Boomers. 1942

Schoolcraft, Henry R[owe]. **Personal Memoirs of a Residence of Thirty Years With the Indian Tribes on the American Frontiers.** 1851

Smalley, Eugene V. **History of the Northern Pacific Railroad.** 1883

[Smith, William Rudolph]. **Observations on the Wisconsin Territory.** 1838

Steele, [Eliza R.] **A Summer Journey in the West.** 1841

Streeter, Floyd Benjamin. **The Kaw:** The Heart of a Nation. 1941

[Switzler, William F.] **Switzler's Illustrated History of Missouri, From 1541 to 1877.** 1879

Tallent, Annie D. **The Black Hills.** 1899

Thwaites, Reuben Gold. **On the Storied Ohio.** 1903

Todd, Charles S[tewart] and Benjamin Drake. **Sketches of the Civil and Military Services of William Henry Harrison.** 1840

Wetmore, Alphonso, compiler. **Gazetteer of the State of Missouri.** 1837

Wilder, D[aniel] W[ebster]. **The Annals of Kansas.** 1886

Woollen, William Wesley. **Biographical and Historical Sketches of Early Indiana.** 1883

Wright, Robert M[arr]. **Dodge City.** 1913